Bardon´s first Steps -

A Commentary

by

Ray del Sole

Success in

Bardon´s first Steps -

A Commentary

ISBN 978-1-4461-8013-6

Attention

Please regard that you take the responsibility for all exercises, experiments and advices you do or follow in this book. All warnings of spiritual teachers, especially by Franz Bardon, Indian Yogis and me should be taken serious. Spiritual training is an art and science and not something to play with or for curiosity. Spiritual development takes years, whole life times, many incarnations indeed. As you are an eternal being you have time enough to proceed step by step keeping the balance in all aspects.

Mastership is the natural result of training. So simple – so true.

Ray del Sole

I dedicate this book to all genuine spiritual seekers and followers of Franz Bardon. May you all find your way to the eternal light and real mastership.

Ray del Sole

TABLE OF CONTENTS

INTRODUCTION

Dear reader,

already for a very long time I have been engaged in spiritual studies and practice. So I certainly know the problems, the misunderstandings and also the obstacles and traps on the path.

I know that it can be hard to get the right access to Bardon´s training. So my aim is to ease your entry in the practical training by showing you hidden aspects of the exercises. In this way you increase your understanding of Bardon´s intelligent training concept and you will be able to master the threshold successfully.

Please regard the things which I have talked about in my book "Preliminary Practice for Franz Bardon´s Initiation into Hermetics". There are already main hints given for a successful access to Bardon´s training.

Certainly it is not my aim to comment all exercises of Bardon but only the first few. When you have stepped in then you will be able to master all following exercises on your own. In addition there are many hints and recommendations for all aspects of Bardon´s training available today. It is just up to you to do the exercises.

In the following chapters I will quote what Bardon says regarding the exercises and steps and I will add my commentaries for a deeper understanding and clarity.

So welcome dear seeker to the real training and to real experiences beyond intellectual discussions.

Ray del Sole

How to use this book

I quote Bardon in cursive letters with "Bardon:" in bold. My comment is in normal letters with "Ray:" in bold. In some cases I omit parts of Bardon's texts which I do not need/want to comment. To mark it I set some points like this...... To keep straight on the quotations I have to divide Bardon's descriptions into parts. So it can be difficult to get the whole original meaning. For a better understanding I recommend to take your "Initiation into Hermetic" book additionally for studying my book. There you can read first the whole description of an exercise by Bardon and then you turn to the quotations with my comments. This should work quite well.

Step I - Introduction

Bardon: *Let us now turn to the practical side of the initiation. We must always be aware of the fact that the body, soul and mind are to be trained simultaneously, for otherwise it would be impossible to gain and maintain the magic equipoise.*

Ray: Body, soul and mind represent the three planes of existence, - the mental plane, the astral plane and the physical/material plane. All three planes are analogue to each other, connected, interdependent and in interaction. To keep balance, health and a safe development all planes/bodies have to be built up simultaneously. There is simply no alternative.

Bardon: *In the theoretic part I already called attention to the dangers possibly rising from one-sided training. It is not advisable to hasten development, because everything needs time. Patience, perseverance and tenacity are fundamental conditions of the development.*

Ray: Everything needs time. Why? Because your mind, soul and body have to adapt themselves to the new and higher activity, to the increased flows of energy, to the spiritual powers. This means that you whole microcosm has to undergo a real and deep transformation, spiritualization. It is similar to transforming a small battery with thin cables into a big battery with high voltage cables. This takes time. The body has to build up new structures to be able to cope with the new strong energies. So indeed it is senseless to hasten or to force progress because your microcosm needs time for changes of energy and structure. To hasten, to put too much pressure means in fact to cause damage and imbalance. This is not good. It is much better and intelligent to increase slowly and smoothly your training, especially the concentration exercises and later the breathing of energy to give your body enough time for transformation. Remember that everything in nature needs time to build up new structures – like fruits and plants in the growing process.

Patience, perseverance and tenacity are the major keys for real success in the spiritual training. They are most important.

Bardon: *The pains taken in one's development will be amply rewarded. Whoever is willing to enter the magic path should regard it as his sacred duty to practice regular exercises.*

Ray: Regular practice is the next important key for success. It has something to do with rhythm, with repetition, with strengthening a habit, also with strengthening mental and astral energies, patterns. It is similar with setting seeds. You must water them daily so that they grow in best way. If you do it from time to time the seeds wouldn´t grow up. Daily care for your development is absolutely necessary. Especially abilities should be "watered" daily until you have mastered them perfectly. They need fresh energies daily to grow.

Beside this regular practice prepares your body in best way for the wished for performance, for accomplishing the exercises. The referring energies are provided as well as the right attitude automatically. This is the same when you do regularly training in sports. Your body longs for the training as it is used to it.

Bardon: *He ought to be kind, generous and tolerant with his fellow men, but relentless and hard with himself. Only such behavior will be followed by* *success in magic. Refrain from condemning or criticizing and sweep your own doorstep first. Do not permit anyone to look into your sanctuary. The magician will always keep silence with respect to his way, rise and success. This silence grants the highest powers and the more this commandment is obeyed, the more easily accessible these powers will become. Manage it so that you spend as much time as possible in your rise or advance.*

Ray: As Bardon says – no pain, no gain! If you want to reap good fruits you must till the field before. Spiritual training can mean hard work. It depends on your personal preparation. People with pure souls, a high maturity and good talents have worked hard in former life times and have an easier access in this life. But at last everyone has to work for his development. Cheating is impossible and a short cut doesn't exist.

Bardon: *It is quite unnecessary to waste time with sitting for hours, drinking beer and passing time in trivial company. Time is running away like water, never to return. A certain amount of time ought to be provided for, but it is very necessary to stick to it. Exceptions ought to be allowed for only in quite inevitable cases. Man is subject to habits, and once accustomed to a definite timetable for his exercises, he will feel compelled to do his exercises. In the same way as there is a want for the necessities of life such as eating, drinking and sleeping, it ought to happen in regard to the exercises which must, as it were, become a habit. This is the sole way to attain a sure and full success. There is no prize without diligence. It is my ambition to arrange for the instructions as if they were meant for the busiest man. He who has plenty of time of hand may be able to be occupied with two or more exercises at the same time.*

Ray: Time is absolutely precious. You are probably not aware of how much you pay with each single incarnation. As you have found the teachings of Bardon you have the great chance to develop yourself without limits. When you spend daily half to one hour for practice and studies and you have maybe at least ten to thirty years left of your life then you can master all three books. Mastership means real freedom and total understanding of creation. As a master you can do everything in best and successful way. Your life becomes a piece of art.

Although time is absolutely precious you also need spare time to meet with friends, family and to follow leisure activities. This is necessary to keep in touch with "normal" people, with the "normal" world and also to balance the demanding, serious magical studies.

Hard training from morning to evening is not possible, not bearable as it would mean overstraining of the whole microcosm. Everything has to follow the laws of balance, health and harmony.

Step I - Magic Mental Training

1. Thought Control, Discipline of Thoughts, Subordination of Thoughts

Bardon: *Take a seat in a comfortable chair or lie down on a settee. Relax the whole body, close your eyes and observe the train of your thoughts for five minutes, trying to retain it. At first, you will find that there are rushing up to you thoughts concerning everyday affairs, professional worries, and the like. Take the behavior of a silent observer toward these trains of thoughts, freely and independently.*

Ray: It is recommendable to take a seat instead of lying down. A vertical position keeps you awake; it supports mental and astral activity, - what you need for all kinds of meditation and concentration. A horizontal position supports passivity, sleep and journeys of mind and soul where the physical body should sleep.
The aim of the exercise in a first step is to differentiate between yourself and the thoughts in your mind; - you are not identical with your thoughts. In fact you will become the master of your thoughts with full control over the quantity and quality of them in your mind.

Bardon: *According to the mentality and the mental situation you happen to be in at the moment, this exercise will be more or less easy for you. The main point is not to forget yourself, not to lose the train of thoughts, but to pursue it attentively.*

Ray: The exercise increases your attentiveness. You become aware of what you think. Attentiveness will be increased through the whole training to highest levels.

Bardon: *Beware of falling asleep while doing this exercise. If you begin to feel tired, stop instantly and postpone the exercise to another time, when you intend not to give in to tiredness. The Indians sprinkle cold water on their faces or rub down the face and upper part of their bodies to remain brisk and not waste precious time. Some deep breathing before you begin will also prevent tiredness and sleepiness. As time goes on, each disciple will find out such little tricks by himself. This exercise of controlling thoughts has to be undertaken in the morning and at night. It is to be extended each day by one minute to allow the train of thoughts to be pursued and controlled without the slightest digression for a time of 10 minutes at least after a week's training. This space of time is destined to the average man. If it should not suffice, everyone can extend it according to his own apperception. In any event, is advisable to proceed very consciously, because it is of no use to hurry, development being quite individual in men. On no account go further before the preceding exercise is perfectly under control. The attentive disciple will realize how, at the beginning, thoughts rush on to him, how rapidly they pass before him so that he will have difficulty to recollect the lot of manifold thoughts. But from one exercise to the next, he will state that thoughts come up less chaotic, moderating little by little, until at last only a few thoughts emerge in his consciousness, arriving, as it were, from a far distance.*

Ray: Here Bardon describes one side effect and aim of this exercise, - the amount of thoughts running through the mind will be/must be reduced to a minimum. This gives peace of mind and clarity. And it also increases your attentiveness; - you are able to perceive much more information in everyday life. In India thoughts are compared with jumping monkeys. They are like chaos in the mind, bothering, confusing. Your mind should be clear and calm like the blue sky or like the calm surface of a lake. Only then you are able to see the ground, God, reality. Think about it.

Bardon: *The keenest attention ought to be given to this work of thought control, as it is very important for magic development, a fact that everyone will realize later on. Providing that the mentioned exercise has been thoroughly worked through and everyone has a complete command of it in practice, let us pass over to the mental training Up to now we have learned to control our thoughts. The next exercise will consist in not giving way in our mind to thoughts obtruding themselves on our mind, unwanted and obstinate. For instance, we must be able not to occupy ourselves any longer with the tasks and worries of our profession when we come home from work and return the family circle and privacy. All thoughts not belonging to our privacy must be set aside, and we ought to manage to become quite a different personality instantly. And just the other way round: in our job, all thoughts have to be concentrated in it exclusively, and we must not allow them to digress or wander home, to private affairs, or elsewhere. This has to be practiced time and again until it has developed into a habit. Above all, one ought to accustom oneself to achieve whatever one does with full consciousness, whether in professional work or in private, regardless whether the point is a big one or a trifle.*

Ray: Thought control means indeed the full control of the amount and quality of the thoughts in your mind. Thoughts should be always useful, positive and analogue to the situation you are actually in. Normal people waste their time with negative thoughts, with thinking about things of the future or the past which have no direct sense. Thoughts mean mental energy and this should be used well.

Bardon: *This exercise should be kept for a lifetime, because it is sharpening the mind and strengthening the consciousness and the memory.*

Ray: One aspect of this exercise is certainly the introspection, the self-knowledge. The thoughts in your mind mirror yourself. So this is an indicator of your actual situation, balance. Negative thoughts and too much thoughts show that there is an imbalance and that a clearing and rebalancing is necessary. You should cultivate always positive, constructive thoughts like beautiful flowers in a garden. Pest plants have to be cleared to keep the beauty and harmony.

Bardon: *Having obtained a certain skill in this exercise, you may turn to the following one. The purpose will now be to hold onto a single thought or idea for a longer while, and to suppress any other thoughts associating and obtruding with force on the mind. Choose for this purpose any train of thoughts or ideation or a suitable presentation according to your personal taste. Hold onto his presentation with all your strength. Vigorously refuse all the other thoughts that have nothing to do with the thoughts being exercised. At first you probably will succeed only for a few seconds, later on for minutes. You must manage to concentrate on one single thought and follow it for 10 minutes at least. If you succeed in doing to, you will be fit for a new exercise.*

Ray: The holding of one thought is the entry exercise of concentration. Here you can certainly choose a thought you prefer, you like. This should make it easier to keep it. All other thoughts have to be neglected, to be kept outside. If you have problems with this then you can use a hidden technique. Imagine that during this exercise no disturbing thoughts are able to enter your mind. Imagine also that you have total control over your thoughts. Meditate upon these two ideas and strengthening them until they have realized. Put will power and belief in these ideas during your meditation; also repeat them several times like it is described later in the autosuggestion chapter. This will help. It is the basic technique for all problems. Always imagine full success in your exercises. Imagine that you are able to master them. Increase and manifest these ideas with will and belief and certainly with repetition and meditation.

Bardon: *Let us then learn how to produce an absolute vacancy of mind. Lie down comfortably on a bed or sofa or sit in an armchair and relax your whole body. Close your eyes. Energetically dismiss any thought coming upon you. Nothing at all is allowed to happen in your mind; an absolute vacancy of mind must reign. Now hold on to this stage of vacancy without digressing or forgetting. At first, you will manage to do so for only a few seconds, but by practicing it more often, you will surely succeed better at it. The purpose of the exercise will be attained if you succeed in remaining in this state for a full 10 minutes without losing your self-control or even falling asleep.*

Ray: Stillness of mind can be mastered in the same way like described before. Meditate upon that you are able to keep this stillness of mind, that absolutely no thoughts are bothering you. Imagine your total success in this exercise. Another access is to set your awareness, your sensation on your crown chakra, - press with your finger tip on the highest center point of your head and then keep your awareness there. This concentration focus will help you to reach stillness of mind.

The hidden aim is to increase your divine guidance, your connection to God with this exercise. Stillness is an aspect of Akasha, of God and indeed God can be found in stillness. In best case you achieve a first, maybe deep enlightenment with this exercise. As a vacuum cannot exist in nature something must fill the vacuum of your mind and this is the spirit of God coming through your crown chakra. A high spiritual attitude for such results is recommendable/ necessary.

In general you will increase your divine intuition and also your ability of perception. You become as clear as the calm surface of the lake or as clear as the blue sky. It is also a preliminary practice for the work with Akasha and with this with the perception of the higher realms, things like clairvoyance etc.

Bardon: Carefully enter your success, failure, duration of your exercises and eventual disturbances into a magic notebook (See details under the heading "Magic Soul Training"). Such a diary will be useful to check your progress. The greater the scrupulousness you use in doing so, the more easily you will undergo all the other exercises. Prepare a working schedule for the coming day or week, and most of all, indulge in self-criticism.

Ray: I recommend here to use at least two or three different notebooks. One to document your success, failures, problems concerning the exercises. A second one to document your spiritual experiences and dreams – like a diary. And a third one to document experiments, instructions for magical operations and special mediations.

It is good to use a PC for such purposes as you are able to work with Excel and Word, to organize your documentation in the best way, also to find things easily by using the research tools. Working plans for weeks are easily made with Excel schedules.

Step I - Magic Psychic Training

1. Introspection of Self-Knowledge
2. Making of the (Black & White) Mirrors of the Soul

Bardon: *In our own mansion, meaning our body and our soul, we must find our way about at every moment. Therefore our first task will be to know ourselves. Each initiation system, no matter which kind it may be, will put this condition in the first place. Without self-knowledge there will be no real development on a higher level. In the first days of psychic training, let us deal with the practical part of introspection or self-knowledge. Arrange for a magic diary and enter all the bad sides of your soul into it. This diary is for your own use only, and must not be shown to anybody else. It represents the so-called control book for you. In the self-control of your failures, habits, passions, instincts and other ugly character traits, you have to observe a hard and severe attitude towards yourself. Be merciless towards yourself and do not embellish any of your failures and deficiencies. Think about yourself in quiet meditation, put yourself back into different situations of your past and remember how you behaved then and what mistakes or failures occurred in the various situations. Make notes of all your weaknesses, down to the finest nuances and variations. The more you are discovering, all the better for you. Nothing must remain hidden, nothing unrevealed, however insignificant or great your faults or frailties may be. Some especially endowed disciples have been able to discover hundreds of failures in the finest shades. Disciples like these possessed a good meditation and a deep penetration into their own souls.*

Ray: At the old oracle of Delphi there was written: "Know yourself and you will know the universe!" This hints at the analogy of the human microcosm with the universe, - macrocosm. Indeed we must know ourselves completely and then we are able to understand the hidden aspects, the true nature of the cosmos. At last we work on becoming similar to the cosmos, to contain all cosmic powers and abilities.

The gaining of self-knowledge starts with the exercise of introspection, with the two mirrors of your soul.

It is very important here to differentiate between the past and the present. Everyone undergoes processes of change and transformation. This means that former negative characteristics or deficits have changed meanwhile into neutral or positive qualities. So in fact when you analyze yourself through the years of your life you will see a development of your personality. Negative characteristics of former days which do not exist any longer are not interesting today. As said already such an analysis shows only your personal development but it has no further meaning. So what really counts is your present situation, your imbalances and problems of today. On these problems you have to work to reach balance and harmony. Certainly you must clear and heal yourself from traumas of your past.

A deep penetration of your soul is good to train your meditation skills. But it makes no sense to practice this endlessly like some students like to.

So the main point here is to get to know yourself, to analyze you actual situation and to be able on this basis to work on clearing, healing and balancing you completely.

A further application is to use the mirrors from time to time to control yourself, - if everything is still in balance or if there is a need to rebalance something. Balance is one main aim of the whole spiritual development, - inner balance, balance with the world your are living in and balance according to the macrocosm and its spiritual nature.

Certainly it makes sense to be 100% honest to yourself without sugarcoating or ignoring of bad habits etc.

Bardon: *Wash your soul perfectly clean; sweep all the dust out of it. This self-analysis is one of the most important magic preliminaries. Many of the occult systems have neglected it, and that is why they did not achieve good results. This psychic preliminary work is indispensable to obtain the magic equilibrium, and without it, there is no regular progress of the development to be thought of.*

Ray: Those who do not this work will be misled and have to fall. Negative characteristics are the worst trap on the path. Beside this Akasha itself will block your progress. Only the pure with the right spiritual attitude are blessed with real understanding and progress. This is a kind of protection function in creation.

Bardon: *Therefore you ought to devote some minutes' time to self-criticism m in the morning and at night. If you have got the chance of some free moments during the day, avail yourself of them and do some intensive thinking, whether there are still some hidden faults anywhere, and if you discover them, record them on the spot so as not to forget a single one.*

Ray: This exercise increases your attentiveness very much as you observe yourself in all kinds of situation if you make any mistakes or if you show negative behavior etc.

Bardon: Whenever you happen to find out any deficiency, do not delay to note it immediately. If within a week you do not succeed in discovering all your faults, spend another week on these inquiries until you have definitely established your list of offences. Having achieved this problem within one or two weeks, you have reached the point to begin with a further exercise.

Ray: Here Bardon says that this exercise should last about one, two or three weeks but not more. Remember time is precious and there is much to accomplish. I know students who do nothing else over years to think about their mistakes. This is not good. This is a waste of time and not productive.

Bardon: Now by intensive thinking, try to assign each fault to one of the four elements. Appoint a rubric in your diary to each element and enter your faults into it. You will not feel sure of which elements some of the faults are to be assigned. Record them under the heading of "indifferent". In the progressing development you will be able to determine the element corresponding to your deficiency. For instance, you will ascribe jealousy, hatred, vindictiveness, irascibility, and anger to the fiery element; frivolity, self-presumption, boating, squandering, and gossiping to the element of air; indifference, laziness, frigidity, compliance, negligence, shyness, insolence, and instability to the watery element; laziness, lack of conscience, melancholy, irregularity, anomaly and dullness to the element of earth. In the following week you will meditate on each single rubric, dividing it into three groups. In the first group you will enter the biggest failures, especially those that influence you strongest or happen at the slightest opportunity. The second group will embrace faults occurring less frequently and in slighter degree. In the last group you are recording those faults that happen only now and again. Go on doing so with the indifferent faults, too.

Ray: This second exercise lets you become familiar with the elements on the astral plane so that you know which element provides a negative or positive quality. You will be able to analyze yourself and other people in shortest time regarding their imbalances and their individual temperaments, - the dominance of one or two elements in their personality. With this ability you can understand people quickly and you can discover analogue characteristics or problems of them in addition. So these are great psychological tools.

Bardon: *Work conscientiously at all times; it is worth while! Repeat the whole procedure with your good psychical qualities, entering them into the respective categories of the elements. Do not forget the three columns here as well. For example, you will assign activity, enthusiasm firmness, courage, and daring to the fiery element, diligence, joy, dexterity, kindness, lust, and optimism to the air element, modesty, abstemiousness, fervency, compassion, tranquility, tenderness, and forgiveness to the watery element, and respect, endurance, conscientiousness, thoroughness, sobriety, punctuality, and responsibility to the earth element. By doing so, you will get two so-called psycho- mirrors, a black one with the evil qualities, and a whit one with the good and noble character traits. These two magic mirrors are correct occult mirrors, and none but the owner has any right to look into them at all. Let me repeat once more that the owner must endeavor to elaborate his magic mirrors precisely and conscientiously. If, in the course of the development, he should remember any good or bad quality, he can still record it under the respective heading. These two magic mirrors will allow the magician to recognize rather exactly which of the elements is prevailing in his black or white mirror. This recognition is absolutely necessary to attain the magic equipoise, and the further development depends on it.*

Ray: Certainly these mirrors are something very private and should be kept secret as they are the key to your personality. On the basis of your analysis you will build the work on refining your microcosm. Your personality will unfold in the four elements to a perfect temple of God.

STEP I - MAGIC PHYSICAL TRAINING

1. THE MATERIAL OR CARNAL BODY

Bardon: *Hand in hand with the inner development of spirit and soul has to go that of the outer, the body also. No part of your Ego must lag behind or be neglected. Right in the morning, after getting up, you will brush your body with a soft brush until your skin turns faintly reddish. By doing so, your pores will open and be able to breathe more freely. Besides, the kidneys are exonerated for the most part. Then wash your whole body or the upper part of it, at least, with cold water and rub it with a rough towel until you feel quite warm. Sensitive people may use lukewarm water, especially in the cold season. This procedure ought to become a day's routine and be kept for a lifetime. It is so refreshing and removes tiredness. In addition to this, you should practice morning gymnastics, at least for some minutes a day, to keep your body flexible. I shall not put up a special program of such gymnastic exercise as everyone can draw it up according to his age and personal liking. What matters most is to keep your body elastic.*

Ray: Here is all said. Your physical body should be trained well as it has to bear great powers later. A weak body can´t cope with strong energies. The body should be in total health and really fit. Basic gymnastics taught by Mantak Chia are really recommendable. They are excellent and described in his book Tao Yoga. Strength training and endurance training are also recommended. Physical fitness is the basis for success in the spiritual training and for success in life. It is certainly also the basis for real health on all three planes.
In a fit body the energies can circulate perfectly. Also the level of vital energy is much higher than the level of normal people.

2. MYSTERY OF BREATHING

Bardon: *Breathing is to be given your very careful consideration. Normally each living creature is bound to breathe. There is no life at all without breathing. It is obvious that a magician ought to know more than the mere fact of inhaling oxygen and nitrogen which the lungs absorb and exhale as carbon dioxide and nitrogen. The lungs cannot exist without breathing and food. All we need for our life, and what preserves our life, to wit, breathing*

and food, is tetrapolar, four elements plus a fifth, the vital element or Akasha principle, as we have said in the theoretical part about the elements.
But the air we are breathing has a finer degree of density than the grossly
material food has. But according to the universal laws, both of them have
the same nature, being tetrapolar and serving to keep the body alive. Let
us therefore return to breathing. Oxygen is subject to the fiery element and
nitrogen to the element of water [or: nitrogen = air; hydrogen = water].
The airy element is the mediating element and the earth element [carbon
or carbon dioxide] is that which holds together the oxygen and the nitrogen.

Ray: The analogy of the elements regarding physical air and breathing is
not important here. Bardon just wants to say that we can observe the
work of the four elements in everything, - also in the physical air. Unfortunately some things became a little bit mixed up by the process of writing
down the book from record tapes. In addition whoever used the brackets
[...] made also mistakes. So originally it was meant that there are two elements, - fire and water which can be observed in the physical air. Oxygen
belongs to the fire element. Hydrogen, nitrogen and carbon belong to the
water element. Remember that air is always a mixture of several gas-
es/chemical elements. So when oxygen reacts with another element then
something new is built, - for example carbon dioxide or water (2x hydrogen + 1x oxygen). Then we have the earth element. The air element describes the character of the connection between oxygen and for example
carbon. And that´s it.
For breathing we need the oxygen of the air, - the fire element for the
active processes in the body and as you know the fire element connects
itself with the water element and carbon dioxide is the result, - what we
exhale. I hope I was able to clear some misunderstandings. It is certainly
not a big or important thing but it is cleared now. By the way, - Bardon
was inter alia a skilled alternative practitioner who managed a hospital at
the end of the Second World War. So you can be sure that he was aware
of the human metabolism.

Bardon: *The Akasha or etheric element is the lawful causal or divine principle. Just as in the great universe of nature, here the elements too have
their polarity, the electric as well as the magnetic fluid. By normal or un-
conscious breathing, the body is supplied only with as much elemental
substance as is necessary for its normal preservation. Here also the supply*

depends on the consumption of elemental substance. It is quite different with conscious breathing. If we put a thought, an idea or an image, no matter whether it's concrete or abstract, in the air to be inhaled, it will take in the Akasha principle of the air concerned and convey it through the electric and magnetic fluids to the air substance. This impregnated air will play a double role when it is conveyed to the lungs through the blood vessels. In the first place, the material parts of the elements are destined to preserve the body; secondly, the electromagnetic fluid, charged with the idea or the image, will lead the electromagnetic air colored with the idea from the bloodstream through the astral matrix to the astral body, and from there to the immortal spirit through the reflective mental matrix. And this is the solution of the secret of breathing from the magic point of view.

Ray: It sounds quite complicated but the main message is that you can combine your natural breathing process with inhaling ideas, images, also feelings, etc. This is used for influencing yourself on mental, astral (soul) and physical plane.

Bardon: *Many theologies utilize conscious breathing for instructive purposes, as for example the Hatha yoga system, without knowing the right process. Several people have suffered severe damage to their health, a fact only to blame in the extreme breathing exercises asked for by this system, especially when such practices have been realized without the guidance of an experienced leader(guru). In most cases, the inexperienced reader has been persuaded to do these exercises because they were promised a quick acquisition of occult powers. If he wants, the magician can achieve this aim much more easily and sooner with the aid of the universal initiating system described so thoroughly in the present book.*

Ray: You will see that most of the magical operations work with breathing energy or in other words with charging all kinds of energy. So the impregnation of normal air is certainly only the access to the art and science of energetic breathing.
I can't recommend Hatha Yoga for real spiritual students who follow high ideals and the path of Bardon. For us it is a waste of time. Hatha Yoga and its meaning are completely misunderstood in the West. Hatha Yoga is in fact just a physical preparation, a preliminary training for real meditative Yoga. When you do "physical preparation" over years and think that you are a Yogi then you have simply missed the point. Hatha Yoga provides in

best case a few benefits for health but it makes more sense to look for a different physical training. Hatha Yoga itself does not provide real magical powers or real enlightenment. This just in short.

Bardon: *Consequently it is quite evident that it is not the quantity of inhaled air that matters, but the quality respecting the idea impregnating the air substance. Therefore it is not necessary nor even advisable to pump the lungs full with a lot of air, putting a needless strain on them. Consequently, you will do your breathing exercises slowly and calmly, without any haste. Sit down comfortably, relax the whole body, and breathe in through the nose. Imagine that with the inhaled air, health, tranquility, peace, success, or everything you are aiming at, will pass into your body through the lungs and the blood. The eidetic image of your idea must be so intense that the air you are inspiring is so strongly impregnated with your desire that it has already become reality. You should not allow the slightest doubt about this fact. To avoid weakening, it will be enough to start with seven inhalations in the morning as well as at night. Increase the number of breaths gradually to one more in the morning and at night. Do not hurry or exaggerate, for everything needs time. In any case, you should not proceed to the imagination of another different desire before the first chosen one has been completely accomplished. In a pupil endowed with talents of a high order, success will manifest itself, at the earliest, after seven days, all depending on the degree of imagination and aptitude. Someone else will need weeks, even moths for the realization of his desires because the kind of desires will also play an important role. It is therefore desirable not to form egotistic wishes to begin with, but to confine them to the abovementioned ones such as tranquility, health, peace and success. Do not extend breathing exercises to more than one-half hour. Later on, a standard ten minutes will do for you.*

Ray: I recommend to see this exercise only as the access to higher practices. So do the training as described and make some experiences with influencing yourself by natural breathing together with inhaling qualities like peace, happiness, etc. It is necessary that you experience how it works and that it works. Later in your training you will do such things more sophisticated and wishes will manifest faster.

3. Conscious Reception of Food

Bardon: *What has been said about breathing applies in the same way to taking nourishment. Here also the same elemental processes are going on as they happened to in the air being inhaled, but the effect of the elements is stronger and more material. Desires impressed on food have a considerable influence on the material plane, where they are exposed to the most material emanations of the elements. Therefore the magician will do well to consider this aspect if he wants to achieve anything concerning his body or other material desires. Now sit down in front of your dish of food that you are going to eat, and with the most intense imagination possible, concentrate on your desire being embodies in the food and as effective as if indeed it had already been realized. If you happen to be alone, undisturbed and not watched by anyone, hold your hands in blessing manner above your food. Not having this opportunity, at least impress your desire upon the food you are taking in, or close your eyes. You may give the impression of saying a prayer before eating your meal, a gesture that is quite true, as a matter of fact. Then eat your food slowly but consciously with the intrinsic conviction that, together with your food, your desire actually is passing into your whole body, down to the finest nerves. The taking of food ought to be a sacred act to you, similar to the communion of Christianity. For the magic constitution it is not advisable to eat in a hurry. All kinds of food and beverages are suitable for the magic impregnation with desires. Yet all the impregnated foods and drinks have to be consumed entirely, and nothing should be left over. Do not read during a meal. Unfortunately a great many people are in this bad habit. Any kind of conversation is also undesirable. One should eat only with the maintenance of one's desire. It is to be noted that no opposite desire should associate. For instance, if you are aspiring after health through conscious or magic breathing, you must not concentrate on success during your meal. It is most advantageous to foster the same desire in breathing as well as in eating to avoid any opposite vibration or emanations in your body. Remember the proverb: "He who chases two hares at the same time will never catch one." Whoever in the conscious reception of food takes example in the Eucharistic mystery, will find an analogy to it here, and remember the words of our Lord Jesus Christ: "Take and eat, for this is my flesh; take and drink, for this is my blood"; he will seize their true and primary meaning.*

Ray: It is probably not easy for everyone to bless his meals. So at least it makes sense to bless one meal/food per day as a sacred ritual with full awareness. You can ask God to bless the food through you, - maybe you feel a strong spiritual energy flow through your crown chakra and your blessing hands. As an alternative you can impregnate your food with your wishes for influencing yourself. This is all up to you.

The saying of Jesus means that by the impregnated, blessed food and wine the spiritual power, energy is assimilated by his disciples. This is comparable with the Indian Abisheka, - a transmission of spiritual consciousness and power – enlightenment. So Jesus transmits his spiritual nature to his disciples by this technique.

4. THE MAGIC OF WATER

Bardon: Water plays one of the most important parts, not only in daily life, being absolutely indispensable for drinking, preparing food, washing, producing steam in factories, etc., but also in our magic development; the water element may prove to be a great factor. As we have already stated in the theoretic al par, the watery element rules magnetism or the attractive force, and it is just this property that we shall utilize in the development of our faculties. All the books dealing with the animal magnetism, emanation of od and so on are acquainted with the fact that water can be magnetized or od-ized.

Ray: You may ask what "Od" is and what it means to "magnetize" something. These are old terms. Od is nothing else but vital energy and when you magnetize something then it means that you transmit vital energy to it. "Animal magnetism" refers to the fact that animals and humans, indeed all beings consist of an electromagnetic system of energy and structure. So you can charge beings with energy for healing purposes. The electromagnetic nature provides some interesting laws which are explained further on.

Bardon: But it is far less known how to enlarge this quality or use it in a different way. Not only water but every kind of liquid has the special property of attracting, and according to the contraction, holding fast, no matter whether good or bad influences be concerned. Therefore we may consider the watery element, especially the material kind of it, as an accumulator. The colder water is, the greater its accumulative capacity. With its full specific weight, namely at 39° F (4° C) above zero, it is most responsive. This notion is not so decisive, for the difference of receptivity of water (or other liquids) up to 43° F (6° C) above zero is so insignificant and so faintly visible that only a thoroughly trained magician can recognize these differences. If by increase of heat, water grows lukewarm; its receptivity is rapidly diminishing. Between 7-99° F (36-37° C) it becomes neutral to magnetism. Attention! Here, our only concern is with the specific properties of the attractive power and its practical value with respect to magnetism which results from the interaction of the elements as an undeniable matter of fact.

Ray: Certainly you do not need a thermometer for working with the attractive, magnetic quality of water. It just should be cold. Cold water with its special qualities can be used like a battery which you charge with energy. You can bind a whish and energy to cold water for your purposes. The cold water keeps it as long as it is cold.

Bardon: *The impregnation (through the Akasha principle present in each substance and consequently in physical water too) with a desire can be operated in any object and at any temperature whatsoever. A piece of bread as well as a hot soup or a cup of coffee or tea might be loaded or charged magically. But this charge does not depend on the accumulative capacity of the water element, but takes place through the causal principle of the fifth power of the elements, and is brought about by the electro-magnetic fluid of the elements concerned. It is important to pay attention to this difference to avoid errors.*

Ray: As Bardon says you can charge also hot water but this does not depend on the attractive, magnetic quality of the water. Indeed you can charge everything you like to.

Bardon: *For instance, it is quite impossible to magnetize a dish of hot soup, because the accumulating power of the water element is balanced or increased by the expansion of the heat present in the water if it rises above 99° F (37° C). The soup, however, can be impregnated with the corresponding desire. Now let us regard the magic of water from the practical side. Every time you are washing your hands, think intensely that by washing, not only do you wipe the dirt off your body, but also the uncleanliness from your soul. Think of failure, trouble, dissatisfaction, illness and the like being washed off and turned over to the water. If possible, wash yourself under the tap so that the dirty water can run off immediately, and at this mo-*

ment think that your weaknesses are flowing off with the water. If you have nothing but a washbowl at your disposal, do not forget to throw away the used water immediately, so nobody else can contact it afterwards. You can also dip your hands into cold water for a little while, and concentrate on the magneto-astral attractive force drawing all weaknesses out of your body and your soul. Be firmly convinced that all failures are passing into the water. You will be surprised at the success of this exercise after a short time. This water also is to be thrown away at once. This exercise is extraordinarily effective if you can manage it in the summer while bating in a river, when the whole body (except for the head, of course) is beneath the water. You can do this exercise the other way around also, by magnetizing the water you are going to use, or by impregnating it with your desire, remaining firmly convinced that through washing the power will pass into your body and the desire will be realized. He who has time to spare can combine both exercises by stripping off all evil in one water (say under the tap or in a separate basin), and then washing himself in another basin with the water impregnated with his desire. In this case, namely the first exercise, you have to use soap when washing off the evil. Female adepts have a third opportunity besides the two fore mentioned possibilities: they will concentrate their magnetism on the fact that the water makes the face and skin look much younger, more elastic and thus more attractive. It is therefore advisable not only to wash the face, but to dip the whole face into the water for some seconds. This procedure is to be repeated at least seven times in one turn. A bit of borax may be added to the water for this purpose. There is a further opportunity given to the magician that ought not to be overlooked. I mean the magnetic eyebath. In the morning the magician dips his face into water that has been boiled on the previous day (using a half- filled water basin) and opens his eyes in the water. He rolls his eyes in the water, repeating this exercise equally seven times. At first, he will have the sensation of a slight stinging in his eyes, but this will disappear as soon as the eyes get accustomed to the exercise. Anyone suffering from weak eyesight may add a thin decoctio n of eyebright (Herba Euphrasia) to the water. This eyebath makes the eyes resistant against changes in the weather and consequently strengthens the visual faculty, improving weak vision, and the eyes become clear and shining. Do not forget respectively to magnetize the water destined to this purpose and to impregnate it with your concentrated wish. Advanced pupils who are training for clairvoyance are offered the opportunity here to promote their clairvoyant faculties. That is all, for the moment, about the material development and training of the body. The time limit for the completion of these exercises is fixed from a fortnight up to one month and is meant for people of average aptitudes. Those who have already practiced concentration and meditation should get along in this space of time. Those who are not yet experienced will have to extend their training period; success depends chiefly on the individuality of the pupil. For the practice, it would be useless for him to pass from one step to the next without having completed the foregoing one in such a way that he is well up in it.

Ray: I recommend here to make experiments with these techniques to experience the effects. You can install a ritual clearing with cool water for everyday use. Maybe you do it by taking a shower or by washing your hands. The purpose is to clear yourself from all kinds of negative influences, negative thoughts and feelings, etc. Imagine that the cool water attracts the negative energies and binds them. So all negative influences and characteristics will vanish in the drain.

Additionally you can use also salt to clear you. Salt has a good clearing effect and it is good to use in a bath tub. Take much sea salt.

Step II - Magic Mental Training

1. Autosuggestion or the Secret of Subconsciousness

Bardon: *Before proceeding to describe the exercises of the second step, let me explain the secret of the subconscious and its practical consequences. In the same way as normal consciousness has its seat in the soul, and is activated by the cerebrum in the body, consequently the head, subconsciousness is a property of the soul, residing in the cerebellum, i.e., the back part of the head.*

Ray: Initiates know that the so called subconsciousness has its astral center at the back of the head. It is called back head chakra and it has several functions. It is the opposite of the Ajna chakra between the eye brows. The Ajna chakra represents the normal consciousness. Again here we witness the play of the polarities. Certainly the main focus lies on the mental and astral plane and with this on the chakras and the psychic functions. It makes not much sense to look for thoughts, - mental energies, in the physical brain.

Bardon: *With respect to the magical practice, let us deal with the study of the psychological function of the cerebellum, consequently the subconscious. In every individual that is in his right senses, the normal sphere of consciousness is intact, i.e., he always and at any time is capable of making use of the functions of normal consciousness. As it results from our investigations, there is no power in the universe nor in man that does not vary between opposites. Hence we may consider subconsciousness as the opposite to normal consciousness. That which in normal consciousness we subsume by the concepts of thinking, feeling, willing, memory, reason, and intellect is reflected in our subconsciousness in a contrary way. Practically speaking, we can regard our subconsciousness as our opponent.*

Ray: I recommend to do not regard your subconsciousness as an opponent. Bardon is certainly correct when he says so but it can provide unhealthy, unwished effects when you do so.
Take his description as a teaching but for your practice take it in this way: Think of your normal consciousness as the fire element, maybe the male or yang part and of your subconsciousness as the water element, the female or yin part. So together both build one good unit. The male part gives an impulse, a wish for example and the female part gets pregnant with this and at last gives birth to your wish.
Indeed try to see them as a positive couple which work together to manifest things, babies.
We have to attain positivity in all aspects. So imagine your subconsciousness as a positive good willing and birth giving part of your mind. Then it will support you in manifesting your wishes. Keep the positive unity of both parts of your consciousness. This is absolutely important!

Bardon: *The incentive or the impulse to all that is undesirable, such as our passions, our failures, our weaknesses, originates just in this very sphere of consciousness. To the pupil now falls the task of introspection to disclose the work of this subconsciousness, according to the key of the elements or the tetrapolar magnet. This is a satisfactory task in as much as the pupil will acquire self- reliance by his own reflection or meditation. Hence, sub-*

consciousness is the incentive of all we do not wish for. Let us learn how to transmute this, so to speak, antagonistic aspect of our ego, so that it not only does no harm, but on the contrary will help to realize our desires. Subconsciousness needs time and space in the material world for its realization, two basic principles valid for all things that have to be transmuted into reality from the causal world. Withdrawing time and space from the subconscious, the opposite polarity will cease to bring its influence to bear upon us, and we shall be able to realize our wishes through the subconscious. This sudden elimination of the subconscious offers the key for the practical use of autosuggestion. If, e.g., we inculcate in the subconsciousness the wish of not giving in tomorrow or any other time, to any of our passions, say smoking or drinking alcohol, subconsciousness will have time enough to put some hindrance, directly or indirectly, in our way. In most of these cases, mainly, in the presence of feeble or underdeveloped willpower, subconsciousness will nearly always succeed in taking us by surprise or causing failures. On the other hand, of we exclude the concepts of time and space from subconsciousness while impregnating it with a desire, only the positive pole of subconsciousness will affect us, normal consciousness being equated, and our impregnate desire must have the success we are expecting. This knowledge and the possibilities related to it, are of the greatest importance for the magical development and have, therefore, to be considered as far as self-suggestion is concerned. The phrasing to choose for autosuggestion must always be expressed in the present or imperative form. You should not say: "I shall stop drinking or smoking or whatever". The correct form is: "I do not smoke, I do not drink", or else, "I do not like smoking or drinking" and so on, according to whatever you wish to suggest in a positive or negative sense.

Ray: In general someone has only problems with his subconsciousness when he lacks of a strong will. So a strong will is the key to manifest in life what you wish for. In the magical training the will power will be increased to the maximum.

There are people who feel bothered by using formulas like "I do not drink." as they contain negative elements. The point here is that only students with a lack of will power eventually have problems with such formulas. When you have a strong will then something like this doesn´t matter. Otherwise you can/should try to create completely positive formulas but this is not always possible.

Maybe you wonder about the instruction to use a formula which is in present tense and which expresses the wished for reality already. As we are magicians we are operating with the manifestation of reality, - of a new wished for reality. This reality is at first a mental image, idea but by using of different techniques it will be wrapped in astral energies to manifest itself down in the material realm. So indeed you must derive everything from the aim you set. Such mental and later astral images will create situations which help to manifest them as a new reality. These things are derived from eternal laws of creation. So they are maybe at the beginning strange but later totally normal and clear.

Bardon: The key or clue to self-suggestion is to be found in the form of the phrasing. It is that which, always and in every respect, has to be considered if you wish to do autosuggestion through subconsciousness. Subconsciousness is acting in the most effective and penetrating way during the night, when man is asleep. In the state of sleep, the activity of normal consciousness is suspended, subconsciousness working in its place. The most appropriate time for autosuggestion receptivity, therefore, is the moment when the body is resting drowsily in bed, i.e., immediately before falling asleep as well as immediately after waking up, when we remain still half-awake. That does not mean that a different time would be quite unsuitable for self-suggestion, but these tow moments are most promising, subconsciousness being most responsive then. That is why the magician will never go to sleep in an emotional attitude such as anger or depression, worries which would have an unfavorable influence in his subconsciousness, going on in the same train of thoughts with which he had fallen asleep. Always go to sleep with peaceful and harmonious thoughts or ideas about success, health and pleasant feelings. Before you practice autosuggestion, make up a small chain of 40 beads. A knotted piece of string also will do fine. This expedient is only meant to avoid counting when you are reiterating the suggestive formula over and over, so as not to divert your attention. This little gadget also will serve to make sure how many disturbances happened when you were practicing concentration and meditation exercises. All you have to do is move a bead or a knot at every interruption. The practical use of autosuggestion is very simple. If you have worded that which you want to achieve in a precise sentence in the present and imperative form, such as: "I feel better and better every day", or "I do not like smoking [or: drinking, &c]", or "I am healthy, content, happy", then you may proceed to the real practice. Immediately before falling asleep, take your string of beads or knots and, whether in an undertone, softly, or in your mind, according to your surroundings, repeat the phrase you have chosen and move one bead or knot at every repetition until you arrive at the end of the string. Now you know for sure that you repeated the formula 40 times. The main point is that you imagine your wish as being realized already and having actual existence. If you do not yet feel sleepy after the 40 repetitions, engage yourself for a while longer with the idea that your wish has been accomplished, and keep doing so until at last you fall asleep with your desire still in mind. You must try to transfer your desire to the sleep. Should you fall asleep while reiterating the formula, the purpose will be achieved. In the morning, when you are not quite up and have some time to spare, you ought to reach for the string of beads and repeat the exercise once more. Some people get up several times during the night to urinate or for some other reasons. If so, they can repeat this exercise as well, and they will attain their desires all the sooner [Editor's note: A more modern practice is to use a repeating tape cassette deck to accomplish this automatically].

Ray: As the editor says you can use a repeating cassette deck or similar things. But I would prefer the traditional method using a string with beads. Why? Because you produce energies by repeating a formula and so the idea becomes stronger and stronger to manifest itself. A cassette player does not produce energies in this form. It just gives suggestions.

I wouldn't use a string with knots. This is not comfortable for the practice. You can buy a mala, a prayer chain with up to 108 beads. The best ones are those with very small beads between the normal beads. It is most comfortable for working with them. Additionally you can get pieces with them you set the amount of beads for counting. If you like you can make such a string with beads on yourself but a wonderful mala is something special.

Bardon: *Now the question arises: what kind of wishes can be accomplished by self suggestion? Principally, every wish can be fulfilled as far as mind, soul and body are concerned, for example: refining of the character, repression of ugly qualities, weaknesses, disorders, recovery of health, removal and promotion of various aptitudes, development of faculties, and so on. Certainly, desires having nothing to do with the personality as lottery numbers and such can never be fulfilled.*

2. Concentration Exercises

A. Visual

B. Auditory

C. Sensory

D. Olfactory

E. Taste

Bardon: *On the first step of our magical mental training, we have learned how to control and master our thoughts. Now let us go on to teach you how to raise the capacity of mental concentration in order to strengthen the willpower.*

Ray: Concentration and will power are analogue and we need both in perfection.

Bardon: *Put some objects in front of you, say, a knife, a fork, a pencil, and a box of matches, and fix your eyes on these objects for a while. Try to remember their shapes and colors exactly. Then close your eyes and endeavor to imagine a certain object plastically, in exactly the same form, as it is in reality. Should the object vanish from your imagination, try to recall it again. In the beginning you will be successful in this experiment only for a few seconds, but when persevering and repeating this exercise, the object will appear more distinct, and disappearance and reappearance will take place more rarely from one exercise to the next. Do not be discouraged by initial failures, and if you feel tired, change to the next object. At the beginning, do not exercise longer than 10 minutes, but after a while you may extend the exercise little by little up to 30 minutes.*

Ray: The time of 30 minutes is analogue to the state of Samadhi. A higher state of concentration/meditation can't be reached. It means concentration in perfection. After a longer training Samadhi is reached faster than in 30 minutes. But therefore your whole microcosm has to adapt itself to the higher flows of energy and the higher activity of the psychic centers. So this comes naturally by training and time.

Bardon: In order to check disturbances, use the string of beads or knots described in the chapter about autosuggestion. Move one bead at every disturbance or interruption. Thus later you will be able to tell how many disorders happened in the course of an exercise. The purpose of the exercise is completed if you can hold onto one object for 5 minutes without any interruptions. If you have gotten to this point, you may pass on to imagining the object with your eyes open. Now the object ought to make the impression of hanging in the air and be visible before your eyes in such a plastic shape as to seemingly be tangible. Apart from the one object you imagined, nothing else of the surroundings must be noticed. Check disturbances with the aid of the string of beads. If you have succeeded in holding on to any object hanging plastically in the air for 5 minutes without the least incident, the task of this exercise has been fulfilled. After the visual concentration, let us make an inquiry about the auditory concentration. At the beginning, the creative imagination has to perform a certain role. It is, as it were, impossible to say, "Imagine the ticking of a clock" or something like that because the concept of imagination generally involves a pictorial representation, which cannot be said about auditory exercises. For the sake of better understanding we ought to say: "Imagine you hear the ticking of a cock". Therefore let us employ this kind of expression. Now imagine that you are hearing the ticking of a clock on the wall. You will succeed in doing so only for a few seconds at the beginning, just as in the previous exercises. But by persisting in your exercise, you will hear the sound more and more distinctly, without any disturbance. The string of beads or knots will be beneficial here also for checking the disturbances. Afterward, try to listen to the ticking of a pocket-watch or a wristwatch, or the chime of bells in various harmonies. You may also practice other auditory concentration experiments such as the sounding of a gong, the different noises of hammering, knocking, scratching, shuffling, thunderclaps, the soft rustling of the wind increasing to the howling of the storm, the tunes of a violin or a piano or other instruments. When doing these exercises, it is most important to keep within the limits of auditory concentration, not allowing for pictorial imagination. Should such an imagination emerge, banish it immediately. The chiming of the bell must never evoke the imagination of the bell itself. This exercise is completed as soon as you are able to keep this auditory imagination for 5 minutes. Another exercise is the sensory concentration. Try to produce the sensations of cold, warmth, gravity, lightness, hunger, thirst, and tiredness, and hold on to this feeling for at least 5 minutes without the slightest visual or auditory imagination. If you have acquired the faculty of concentration in such a degree as to be able to produce any sensation you like and hold it fast, you may pass on to the next exercise. Now let us throw some light upon the olfactory concentration. Imagine that you are smelling the scent of various flowers such as roses, lilacs, violets or other perfumes, and hold on to this imagination without allowing a pictorial image of the respective flower to emerge. Try to practice with disagreeable smells of different kinds. Exercise this kind of concentration until you are able to imaginarily bring about any scent at will and keep it for at least 5 minutes. Our last exercise will deal with the taste concentration. Without thinking of any food or drink or without imagining the same, you have to concent rate on taste. Choose the thumping sensations of taste such as sweet, bitter, sat and acid to begin with.

Ray: There are people who think that they have to regard the different zones of sensation of the tongue for this exercise. This is nonsense. The aim is to activate the astral tongue as a sense organ as imagination happens on the astral plane and not on the physical plane. On the higher planes sensation is not bound to time and space. So just focus on your tongue as a whole and in your exercise just on the taste.

Bardon: *Having got some certain skill herein, you may carry out an experiment on the taste of divers spices, at your discretion. If you have succeeded in producing any sensation of the chosen taste and holding onto it for at least 5 minutes, the purpose of this exercise is fulfilled. One or another trainee will meet with smaller or greater difficulties in practicing these concentration exercises. This means that the cerebral function with respect to the concerned taste has been neglected or imperfectly developed. Most of the teaching systems will pay attention only to one or two, or three functions at best. Concentration exercises performed with all the five senses strengthen your mind, your willpower, and you learn not only how to control all senses, but also to develop and finally tem perfectly. A magician's senses must all be developed equally, and he must be able to control them. These exercises are of paramount importance for the magical development, and therefore should never be omitted.*

Ray: These exercises are very important and also very demanding. For a better understanding and also a successful realization I put in here an article of me:

The development of imagination with all senses is probably one of the hardest challenges in the beginning of the spiritual training of Bardon. I want to put some light on this topic for a better understanding and a strategy how it can be accomplished.

The development of the ability to imagine with all senses in the beginning of the magical training has some more or less hidden aims. Imagination is the ability to create on the mental and on the astral plane and later with clear effects on the material plane. The main point here is creation and to be able to create. God is the creator and we as his children are creators too. Without training we are in most cases not good in creating, - not professional. So the ability to create must be refined and strengthened according to our high aim of becoming a true son/daughter of God. The ability to create like God does, shows itself in form of the five senses seeing (fire), hearing (air), feeling (water), smelling (earth) and tasting (earth). The five senses represent five different aspects of energy and matter (matter is just a dense form of energy). So indeed we can create something with a focus on one sense or in best way by regarding the main senses or all. The result is a real created object/being on the mental or astral plane. On the material plane we need our physical body, hands to create something but on the higher planes we create with our senses, with mind, will and belief. For the spiritual development and the whole magical work the ability to create, to imagine is absolutely necessary and this already short after the beginning of the training. This is one aspect.

The next aspect is that creation/imagination is an active process. Exercises which build up our imagination skills are of an active nature. So they are very useful in the beginning of the training where a major aim is to activate the whole microcosm of the student. The senses are very close to the mind, to the mental realm, to the spirit. So when you train your senses then you train and activate your spirit, your mental body/aspect. In the spiritual development all activation processes should start from the spirit, from the mental plane. And this is true for Bardon´s path. So in fact the exercises with the senses have the aim to activate the spirit, the mental plane in your microcosm. As the senses are analogue to the four elements the exercises activate the four elements on the mental plane, later also on the astral plane. This means that the four elements are strengthened and refined by the work with the senses. Analogue to this also the centers/chakras of the senses and the referring brain areas are activated, strengthened and refined. So the whole mental body, mind is cultivated.

This mental activation together with the refinement and strengthening of the four elements on the mental plane is one major, more or less hidden aim. The obvious aim is the refinement of the ability to create with all five senses.

Let´s go to the next points. What means imagination? Imagination is the concentration and forming of energy with focus on one or more senses. And what means concentration? Concentration means to densify energy. So this means when you do an imagination exercise you are at first on a mental plane with for example the idea of a fragrance. The longer you focus on this idea the denser it becomes so that you can really smell it. When you increase your concentration then the fragrance become denser down to the astral plane and maybe so dense that also other people can smell it. This is indeed in main a matter of will/concentration power and time. And here you can see already one sticking point – if you do not keep your concentration long and strong enough then the fragrance can´t manifest/densify itself to be smelled. So imagination and concentration have something to do with your ability to manifest, to densify energies analogue to the used senses. Masters of imagination with a strong will and belief are able to densify mental and astral ideas/objects down to the material realm where others can experience them. This creative ability is certainly as everything else just a matter of training.

What does this all mean for the training itself?

As we have seen there are several different aspects regarding the ability, the exercises and aims. I guess that it is very hard if you follow the pure instructions as Bardon describes them. If you are not blessed with good talents in imagination already then these exercises can be the point where you stop your training because of no real progress. This can be seen as a test if you want to accomplish the spiritual path at all costs or if you do it just for curiosity.

Regarding the different aspects we can divide this training into parts:

- First part (Quantity aspect): We have to activate the centers/ chakras/ sense organs/ brain areas. This means to increase the flow of energy and the activity of the chakras and nadis. It means also the strengthening and refinement of the four elements on the mental level.
- Second part (Quality aspect): We have to train the imagination with all senses with real training objects (pictures/ fragrances/ feelings etc.)

In fact the ability itself, second part is based on the first part. This means that at first you must activate, strengthen and refine your senses and everything which is analogue to be able to use them for higher purposes like imagination and later perception over time and space (clairvoyance etc.).

When we regard and respect this fact then we can divide the training into a first part and in a second one.

First part of the training:

As said already this part has the aim to activate, strengthen and to refine the senses, the sense organs, the analogue chakras and nadis, and the brain areas. This takes place especially on the mental and astral plane with effects also on the physical plane.

The exercise is quite simple but also highly effective. We respect here the balance of the four elements. Take your asana as usual; set your egg timer on three or seven minutes. Then start with fire: Lead your awareness to the Ajna chakra, the point between your eye brows and to your eyes. Keep your feeling, your consciousness and concentration especially on the Ajna but also on your eyes. Hold it for the time of your egg timer. In this way you activate the centers of the fire element, of seeing (and visual imagination. Certainly you will experience side effects like increasing of your will and you concentration ability. In the next round you focus on your ears and on your third eye, forehead chakra, the center point of your forehead, - air element. Third round – focus on your navel chakra (navel) and on your soma chakra (a few centimeters above the forehead chakra at the hairline), - this is good for your ability to feel, - water element. Last round – you focus on your nose and on your tongue, - earth element. Altogether these are 12 or 28 minutes. It is certainly advisable to start with only a few minutes and to increase the time over weeks and months. Too much work on your senses/chakras is not good. You must take much time so that your body, your organs etc. can adapt themselves to the new, higher energy and activity. So maybe you take three or seven minutes for one month and then you increase the time. You should feel well with these exercises. Strong headaches are a sign that you do to much. If you feel uncomfortable then take a break. Do everything slowly and smoothly. Later you can increase the time of training so that you work on two senses per day and then maybe only one sense per day. Just regard the sequence of fire (eyes) – air (ears) – water (feeling) – earth (nose, tongue) to keep the balance of the four elements. You can increase the time up to thirty minutes per sense like Bardon recommends.

After maybe one month or two or three of daily training you will experience that your mental and astral sense organs are good developed. This means that you are able to work with them on the higher planes in an active way – imagination and probably also already in a passive perceptive way, for example clairvoyance. This means you are able to perceive impressions from the higher realms. So when you experience that you are able to gain results then you can start with step two, to refinement and training of imagination itself.

(In general you will experience many different side effects which are all very positive for your spiritual development. Clearing and healing are also aspects.)

Second part of the training:

Your senses, sense organs and brain areas are activated, strengthened and refined so that you are able to work successfully with your senses in an active way on the mental and astral plane. Now you look for training objects which you like, where you can draw your attention easily to, objects you eventually know for a long time.

Examples:

Fire – eye:

Portraits of gods, goddesses, holy symbols, flowers, technical objects, nature elements, etc.

Air – ear:

Spiritual bells, holy chants, mantras, elements from nature, etc.

Water – feeling:

The coolness of water, the heat of a summer day, heavy and dense like a stone, airy and light like a balloon, etc.

Earth – nose:

Fragrances of flowers, of sandalwood, olibanum, of incense sticks, of temples, of nature, etc.

Earth – tongue:

The taste of good chocolate, sweets, common meals, spicery, etc.

Here the training works like Bardon describes it. You take one object, watch it and then you imprint it into your memory to imagine it afterwards. Change the object as often as you like until you achieve full mastership with all single senses. Regard here the sequence in the same way as before.

At first you do the exercises with closed eyes and later with open eyes. And much later with several senses at once. Please have in mind that it is still the mental/astral plane where your imagination takes place and not the material plane. This means it makes no sense to force your physical eyes etc. to manifest physical picture. Your mind is able to crossfade pictures etc. from different planes.

It is possible that some exercises are easier for you than others. Certainly you must bring all on the same level. Thanks to the first part of the training this should have been done already or should be no problem in the second part. You can increase the work/time with the sense where you have problems.

You will also experience that this training will support the work with the elements on the astral plane later. The training with the senses provides indeed a mental mastership over the four elements which makes the astral work easier.

Take your time for the training. You will experience many fascinating results. It is quite equal if this training takes one or three of maybe more months. I guess that most students should be able to get good results within three months.

At last – don´t forget to dissolve your imagined object. Dissolve it like all other energies as you know it from your training.

Don´t imagine things which come along with desires and also no people which you know.

When you have a closer look on my explanations then you can see that I have used some keys of wisdom, - the twofold and the fourfold key. It is quite useful when you understand an exercise and its function and hidden aims. Then you are able to divide it in accomplishable parts.

Be blessed with joy and full success!

Ray

Step II - Magic Psychic Training

1. Magic-Astral balance with respect to the Elements
2. Transmutation or Refinement of the Soul

a. By fight or control

b. By auto-suggestion

c. By transmutation

Bardon: *In the first phase, the pupil has learned how to practice introspection. He has recorded his good and bad properties in accordance with the four elements, and has divided them in three groups. In this way he has made two soul mirrors, a good (white) one and a bad (black) one. These two soul mirrors represent his psychic character. Now he must find out from these records which elemental powers are prevailing in him on the good as well as the evil side, and endeavor to establish the balance of these elemental influences at all events. Without a balance of the elements in the astral body or in the soul, there is no possible magical progress or* *rise. Consequently, in this step we must establish this psychic equipoise. If the novice magician possesses a sufficient amount of willpower, he may pass on to master the passions or qualities that exercise the greatest influence on him. Should he not own a sufficiently strong volition, he may start from the opposite side by balancing small weaknesses first, and fighting greater faults and weaknesses bit by bit until he has brought them under control. The scholar is offered three possibilities for mastering the passions: 1. Systematical utilization of autosuggestion in the way we described previously. 2. Transmutation of passions into the opposite qualities, attainable through autosuggestion or through repeated meditations on and continuous assurance of the good qualities. 3. Attention and volition. By using this method, you will not allow for any outbreak of the passion, fighting it right in the bud. This method is the most difficult and is appropriate only for people possessing a good deal of volition, or willing to achieve a strong willpower by fighting against their passions. If the novice has enough time on hand and wishes to advance as fast as possible in his development, he may use all three methods. The most profitable way is to orient all methods toward one single direction, for example conscious eating, magic of water, and so forth. Then success will not be far off. The purpose of this step is to balance the elements in the soul. The scholar therefore ought to quickly and surely endeavor to get rid of those passions that hinder him most from being successful in the magic art. Under no circumstances should he start with exercises belonging to the steps ahead before being absolutely possessed with the exercises of the second step and having booked a sweeping success, especially in balancing the elements. The refinement of character should be aspired after during the entire course, but as early on as this level, faults and bad qualities that handicap development ought to be eradicated.*

Ray: The presented techniques have the hidden aim to strengthen your will and other analogue qualities in yourself. The will can be strengthened also by concentration exercises and by concentrating on your Ajna chakra, the center of will. This is all up to you. Imbalances of your soul can be cleared and healed also by the use of Bach flowers and a homeopathic treatment.

Indeed all this is not really a matter in which way you accomplish it but that you make it successfully. You must reach balance and you must increase your will power at all costs.

It is absolutely necessary that you get rid of all evil/ negative habits, thoughts, emotions and patterns of behavior. In the coming steps you will work with vital energy and the four elements. When you do this training then negative characteristics can be strengthened, - if you are not already cleared and balanced so far. In fact imbalances and negative qualities provide the biggest obstacles on the path. This is really important to be aware of.

STEP II - MAGIC PHYSICAL TRAINING

1. CONSCIOUS PORE BREATHING
2. CONSCIOUS POSITION OF THE BODY
3. BODY CONTROL IN EVERYDAY LIFE, AT WILL

Bardon: *The tasks of the magical training of the body according to Step I must be retained and ought to become a daily habit, such as washing with cold water, rubbing the body from head to toe, athletic exercises in the morning, magic of water, conscious breathing and so forth. The second step training of the body orders a change of the breathing exercises. In the previous step, we have learned how to breathe consciously and convey the desire inhaled together with the air (through the Akasha principle) to the blood stream via the lungs. In this chapter I am going to describe the conscious pore breathing. Our skin has a double function, i.e., the breathing and the secretion. Therefore we may consider the skin as a second piece of lungs and as a second kidney of the body. Everybody will understand now, for which important reason, we have recommended dry-brushing, rubbing, washing with cold water and all the other directions. First of all, this was intended to exonerate our lungs completely and our kidneys partially, and secondly to stimulate the pores to greater activity. It is certainly super-*

fluous to explain how very profitable all this is for the health. From the magic point of view, conscious pore breathing is of the utmost interest for us, and therefore we shall immediately pass on to practice. Sit down comfortably in an armchair or lie down on a sofa, and relax all your muscles. Try to think that, with each inspiration, not only your lungs are breathing, i.e., inhaling air, but the whole body is doing so. Be firmly convinced that, together with your lungs, each single pore of your body simultaneously receives vital power and conveys it to the body. You ought to feel like a dry sponge which, when dipped into water, sucks it in greedily. You must have the same feeling when breathing in. This way the vital power will pass from the etheric principle and your surroundings to yourself.

Ray: Here is the main point that you do not breathe with you physical body but with your astral body. So indeed the vital energy flows from all directions into your astral body which has the same form like your physical body and certainly you can feel how the energy enters through the surface of your skin, - but this is an astral sensation, not a physical one.

The astral body is not as dense as the physical body, so energy can easily access your astral body and you can charge yourself with energy. The whole breathing exercise depends on your imagination. So what you imagine will happen. Just add to your imagination will power and belief. After some tries you will probably be able to feel the vital energy. This form of energy is simply everywhere so that it is not a problem to get it or to breathe it in. Just try. One main point here is that you focus on the vital energy, that you adjust yourself to this energy like you switch to a wished for channel on TV. Then you receive what you are looking for. So it is a matter of intention.

The breathing of energy is added to the natural breathing of your lungs. So everything should be easy and without straining.

Bardon: *According to his character, each individual will feel this entering of vital power through the pores in a different manner. When, after a certain amount of time and repeated exercises, you are skilled in inhaling through the lungs and with the whole body simultaneously, connect the two breathing methods to your desire inhaling, i.e., breathing in health, success, peace, mastering of passions, or whatever you need most urgently. The fulfillment of your desire (imparted in the present and commandment moods) is to be realized not only through the lungs and the bloodstream but through your whole body. If you have attained a certain skill in this* *experiment, you may also influence exhaling magically by imagining that, at each breathing out, you are secreting the opposite to your desire such as weakness, failure, trouble, and so on. If you have succeeded in exhaling and inhaling through your lungs and whole body, this exercise is completed.*

Ray: Later you will be able to charge yourself with energy independent from your natural breathing. This is then just a matter of will.

Bardon: *The next exercise will deal with the control of your body. It needs a great skill to sit quietly and comfortably, and therefore it is necessary to learn how to do it. Sit down on a chair, in such a way that your spine remains straight. At the beginning, you are allowed to lean back on the chair. Hold the feet together so that they form a right angle with the knees. Sit relaxed, without any stain other muscles, both your hands resting lightly on your thighs. Set an alarm clock to sound off after 5 minutes. Now close your eyes and watch your whole body. At first you will notice that the muscles are becoming restless in consequence of the nervous stimulus. Force yourself as energetically as you can to persevere to sit quietly. However easy this exercise seems to be, as a matter of fact it is rather difficult for a beginner. If the knees tend to separate constantly, you may tie them together with a string to begin with. If you are able to sit without jerking and any special effort for 5 minutes, each new exercise is to be extended one minute longer. If you have managed to sit for at least 30 minutes quietly, comfortably and without any trouble, this exercise will be finished. When you have arrived at this point, you will state that there is no better position for the body to relax and to rest. Should anyone wish to use these exercises of physic carriage for the purpose of developing the will-power, he may make out various carriages at his own discretion, provided he is able to sit relaxed and comfortable without any disturbance at all for a full hour. The Indian yoga system recommends and describes quite a lot of such positions (asanas), asserting that one may win various occult powers by mastering them. It must be left undecided whether it is on the strength of these asanas that such powers are set free. We need a certain position for our magical development, no matter which one, the simplest being that which we described above. It is meant to reassure the body and strengthen the will-power. The main point will always be that mind and soul are in need of an undisturbed action of the body, a problem to be discussed in special exercises further on.*

Ray: As Bardon says it, the main purpose is to give the physical body a good position where it can rest while soul and mind are highly active, - busy with meditation and concentration. So in fact meditation does not mean to be in a sleepy and dull state like many western "Yogis" believe in. In meditation we do not need the physical body as we work on the astral and mental plane. Bardon describes the best position - asana - which is available. So I recommend this asana too and disadvise from strange and demanding Hatha Yoga asanas. Certainly it makes sense to keep one asana for all times as the body becomes accustomed to it and deeper meditation states are supported naturally.

Bardon: *Those scholars who become very tired, mentally as well as psychically in performing the exercises of the first and second steps, and fall asleep regularly during the concentration and meditation exercises, will do best practicing them in the before mentioned position. The beginner ought to practice this sort of body control in his everyday life. He will find a great deal of opportunity by observation and attention. For example, if you feel tired, force yourself to do something else, in spite of your tiredness, irrespective of this being any hobby or a short walk. If you feel hungry, put off the meal for half an hour; if you feel thirsty, do not drink on the spot, but wait for a while. Being used to hurrying all the time, try to act slowly and the other way around. Anyone who is slow should make a point of working fast. It is entirely up to the scholar to control and force body and nerves by willpower. This is the end of the second step exercises.*

Ray: By following these instructions you will experience that you have total control over your body. You are the real master of your microcosm. This is important to experience. It is certainly not the aim to punish yourself with forms of asceticism or to neglect good things in life. Mastership is the aim and mastership means full awareness and control in every situation.

Bardon: *Exercises concerning the elimination of thoughts (negative state) are continued and deepened here.*

Before falling asleep, the most beautiful and purest ideas are to be taken along into the sleep.

Step III - Magic Mental Training

1. Concentration of Thoughts with 2 or 3 Senses at Once
2. Concentration on Objects, Landscapes, Places
3. Concentration on Animals & Human Beings

Bardon: *Knowledge, daring, volition, silence: these are the four pillars of Solomon's temple, i.e., the microcosm and the macrocosm upon which the sacred science of magic is built. According to the four elements, they are the fundamental qualities which must be inherent in each magician if he aspires to the highest perfection in science. Everyone can acquire magic knowledge by diligence and assiduity, and mastery of the laws will lead him, step by step, to the supreme wisdom. Volition is the aspect of will-power that can be obtained by toughness, patience and perseverance in the holy science, and chiefly in its practical use. He who does not intend to satisfy his sheer curiosity only, but is in earnest willing to enter the path leading to the loftiest heights of wisdom, must possess an unshakeable will. Daring: he who is not afraid of sacrifices nor hindrances, indifferent to other people's opinions, who keeps his objective firmly in his mind, no matter whether he meet with success or with failure, will disclose the mystery. Silence: The braggart who is talking big and exhibiting his wisdom will never be a genuine magician. The true magician will never make himself conspicuous with his authority; on the contrary, he will do anything not to give himself away. Silence is power. The more reticent he is about his knowledge and experience, without segregating himself from other people, the more he will be awarded by the Supreme Source. Who aims at acquiring knowledge and wisdom may do his utmost to obtain the aforesaid four fundamental qualities for nothing at all will be achieved in holy magic without these requirements. Now will follow the third step exercises.*

Ray: I recommend to meditate over a good period of time about these four pillars to understand them deeply and integrate them as powers and qualities into your personality. If you like you can develop signs, symbols and maybe rituals referring to these pillars to strengthen and to charge them for a complete manifestation on mental and astral plane with an analogue behavior on the physical plane. This is all up to you and can be quite individual. You can also put it in form of autosuggestive formulas. Think about that you are a temple of God.

In the second grade course, we have learned to practice sensorial concentration by training each sense. On this step, we shall widen our concentration power, expanding from one sense to two or three senses at once. I shall quote some examples, with the help of which the skilled student will be able to arrange his own sphere of action. Imagine plastically a clock hanging on the wall with its pendulum swinging to and fro. Your imagination must be so perfect and so constructive as if it were there, indeed and factually, a clock hanging on the wall. Hang on to this double imagination of seeing and hearing for five minutes. In the beginning, you will succeed in doing so for seconds only, but by means of frequent repetition you will be able to hold on to your imagination for a longer while. Practice makes perfect. Repeat this experiment with a similar object such as a gong, of which you must hear not only the sound but also see the person sounding it. Or try to imagine you see a brook and hear the rustling of the water. Or a cornfield stirred by the wind and you are listening to the whispering of the breeze. Now try for a change and look for similar experiments, arranging them so that two or more senses are affected. Other experiments with optical and acoustic imageries may be composed, e.g., where the eyes and tactual senses (sense of touch) are engaged. All your senses have to be quickened and trained for concentration. You should make a special point of seeing, hearing and feeling, all of which is indispensable for progress in magic. I cannot emphasize enough the high significance these exercises have for your development as a magician. Practice such exercises carefully and daily. If you will be able to hold on to two or three sense concentrations at the same time for at least five minutes, your task will be accomplished. If you begin to feel tired during the concentration exercises, stop and cease to go on. Postpone the exercises till a more favorable moment when you feel mentally and physically fit. Beware of falling asleep during an exercise. Experience has shown early morning hours to be most suitable for concentration work. As soon as you have attained a certain skill in the preceding concentration exercises, and if, consequently you are capable to engage two or three senses at one time for at least five minutes, you may go on. Choose a comfortable position again which for all concentration work is absolutely necessary. Close your eyes and form an imaginary pic-

ture in full plasticity of a well known country place, village, house, garden, meadow, heath, wood, etc. Hold onto this imagery. Every trifling detail such as color, light and form is to be kept exactly in mind. All that you are imagining ought to be modeled in such plastic forms as to allow you to touch them, as if you were present there in fact. You must not let anything slip; nothing should escape your observation. If the image becomes blurred or is about to vanish, recall it again and all the more distinctly. If you have managed to hold the plasticity of the picture fast for at least five minutes, the task is achieved. Next let us try to apply the auditory concentration to the same imagery. Perhaps you were imagining a wonderful forest; listen then at the same time to the warbling of the birds, the murmuring of the brook, the rustling of the wind, the humming of the bees and so on. If you succeed in one imagery, try a similar one. This exercise will be fulfilled as soon as you are able to imagine any region, place or spot you like and engage two or three senses at once for five minutes. If you have reached this degree of concentration, try to do the same exercise with your eyes open, whether fixing your look at one definite point or staring into vacancy. The physical surroundings then must no longer exist for you, and the imagery you choose is to appear floating in the air before your eyes like a fata-morgana. When you are able to hold such imagery fast for five minutes exactly, you may choose another one. The exercise is to be regarded as fully completed if you are able to produce any imagery you like with your eyes open and keep it, with one or several senses, for five minutes. In all of your further concentration exercises, you ought to proceed in the same way as, after reading a novel, when you unfold the images of the single events in your mind. We have learned how to form representation of places and localities we know and have already seen before. Now let us try to imagine localities we have never seen before in our life. At first, we shall do it with our eyes closed, and if we succeed in doing so with two or three senses at once for five minutes, let us do it with eyes open. The exercise is fully completed if we have indeed managed to keep this imagination for five minutes with our eyes open. Now let us pass over from inanimate objects to living creatures. We shall imagine various animals such as dogs, cats, birds, horses, cows, chickens, etc., plastically as we did before with our concentration. Practice with your eyes closed, for five minutes, and later on with your eyes open. Mastering this exercise, imagine the animals in movement, such as a cat washing itself, or catching a mouse, drinking milk, or a dog barking, a bird flying, and so forth. The scholar may choose such or similar scenes at his own liking, first with his eyes closed, and later

on with them open. If you manage it for five minutes without any distur-
bance, the purpose is fulfilled and you may go on to the next exercise. Now
concentrate on men in the same kind of way. Start with friends, relatives,
or acquaintances. Deceased people, and later imagine strangers you never
saw before, first their features only, then the whole head and finally the
fully dressed body, always beginning with your eyes closed and opening
the after a while. You must have reached a minimum of five minutes be-
fore you pass over to the next exercise, dealing with men in their move-
ments such as walking, working, talking, etc. If you have noticed a success
with one sense, say visually, add another sense, e.g., auditory imagination
so that you can hear the individual talking, and imagine his voice. Always
endeavor to adapt imagination to the reality, e.g., the modulation of the
voice, slow or fast speech, just as the person of your imagination actually
does or did. Practice first with eyes closed, then with the eyes open. If you
have booked any success in this field too, concentrate your imagination on
quite strange people, retaining their different features and voices. They
may be people of both sexes and of any age whatsoever. After that, im-
agine people of other races, women, men, young and old, children, e.g.,
Negroes, Indians, Chinese, Japanese, etc. Make shift with books or maga-
zines. Visits to a museum can also do for this purpose. Having managed all
this and keeping the imagination for five minutes with the eyes closed as
well as open, your magic mental training of the third step will be complete.
All these exercises have required perseverance, patience, persistence and
toughness to cope with the enormous difficulties of the task. But those
scholars who master them will be very satisfied with the powers they won
through these concentration exercises. The next step will teach them how
to deepen these powers. Such concentration exercises do not only streng-
then the willpower and the concentrative faculty, but all the intellectual
and mental forces, lifting the magic capabilities of the mind on a higher
level, and besides, they are indispensable as a preliminary practice for
thought transference, telepathy, mental wandering, television, clair-
voyance, and other things more. Without these faculties, the magic disciple
will never get on. Therefore you ought to make every effort to work care-
fully and conscientiously.

Ray: This exercise is certainly also very demanding but when you have
mastered the first exercises of imagination then these new ones are just a
matter of time and training. Important is that you have mastered the entry
in these skills. Then everything is accomplishable.

Step III - Magic Psychic Training

1. Inhaling of the Elements in the Whole Body

A. Fire

B. Air

C. Water

D. Earth

Bardon: *Before starting on the training for this step, the astral equipoise of the elements in the soul has to be established by introspection and self-control unless you wish to do mischief to yourself. If it is absolutely sure that none of the elements is prevailing, you ought to keep working on the refinement of the character, in the course of the development, but you might as well go on to work with the elements in the astral body.*

Ray: As said before it is absolutely necessary that you have full control of yourself and that you have cleared, healed and balanced yourself to a good degree. Negative characteristics and a lack of control are keep the door closed for progress. Perfection is not expected but you must be cleared and in full control over yourself.
The work with the four elements will refine, clear, heal and strengthen your whole personality on all three planes. It means true transformation and spiritual growth.

Bardon: *The task of this step will be to acquire the basic qualities of the elements, producing and dissolving them in the body at will. We are already acquainted with the theory of the action of the elements. Let us deal with the practice: Fire, with its expansion or extendibility in all directions, has the specific quality of heat, and therefore is spherical. Let us then, first of all, acquire this quality and produce it at will in the body as well as in the soul. In body-control we chose an attitude allowing us to remain in a comfortable position, free of any disturbance; Indians call this position asana. For the sake of better understanding, we shall also use this expression* *henceforth. Take the asana position and imagine yourself in the centre of the fiery element which, in the shape of a ball, envelops the universe. Imagine all around you, even the entire universe being fiery.*

Ray: Certainly you do not need to imagine the whole universe. The main point here is to imagine you into the center of an endless space filled with an element. So in fact there is nothing but you surrounded by the element energy. The point here is to connect to the universal element like I compared it with the vital energy and choosing a TV channel.

Bardon: *Now inhale the fire element with your nose and, at the same time, with your whole body (pore-breathing). Draw deep breaths regularly, without pressing air or straining the lungs. The material and the astral body ought to resemble an empty vessel into which the element is being inhaled or sucked in with each breath. This heat ought to grow more and more intense with every breath. The heat and the expansion-power must become stronger, the fiery pressure higher and higher, until you feel yourself at last fiery red hot. This whole process of inhaling the fiery element through the body is, of course, a purely imaginary occurrence and should be exercised with the utmost plastic imagination of the element. Start on seen times inhaling the fire element and increase each exercise by one breathe more. An average of 20-30 breaths will do. Only physically strong pupils of great willpower are allowed to exceed his number at discretion. Use the string of beads again to spare counting the breaths by moving one bead with each inhalation. In the beginning the imaginary heat will be perceived psychically only, but with every repeated experiment, the heat will become physically as well as psychically more perceptible. From a rise of temperature (outbreak of perspiration) it can actually increase to a fever.*

Ray: Interesting is maybe that the astral plane with its energies and perception is more a part of what we call material world as you might think. So what we perceive as material belongs in parts in fact to the astral plane. This is especially true for perceiving heat, cold, airiness and heaviness. You will experience this by working with the elements.

Bardon: *Once the scholar has managed to establish the balance of the elements in the soul, such an accumulation of elements in his body can do him no harm. Having finished the exercise of imaginary accumulation of* *the fiery element, you will, through imagination, feel the heat and the expansion of the fire, and now you may start on the exercise in the opposite succession, inhaling the fire element normally through the mouth and exhaling through it and through the whole body (pore breathing) into the universe again. The number of breaths done when exhaling the element has to correspond exactly to the number of inhalations. For example, if you begin with seven inhalations of the fire element, you must also exhale seven the element seven times. This is very important, because after finishing the exercise the scholar should have the impression that not the smallest particle of this element has remained in him, and the sensation of heat it produced in him must disappear. Therefore it is advisable to use the string of beads for breathing in as well as breathing out. Do the exercises with the eyes closed at first, and then with open eyes. The Tibetan explorer and traveler Alexandra David-Neel in her books a similar experiment practiced by lamas under the name of tumo, which is, however, very imperfect for practical purposes for Europeans and not at all suitable for any student of magic. In the Orient, there are adepts who perform this exercise for years and are able to condense the fire element to such a degree that they walk about naked and barefoot even in the winter without being affected by the cold; they can, indeed, in just a few minutes, dry wet sheets which they wrap around their bodies. By accumulating the fire element, they affect even their environs, which means the surrounding nature as well, so that they succeed in melting snow and ice not only around themselves, but at a distance of kilometers. Such and similar phenomena can be produced by a European also if he can afford the necessary time for it. For our progress in magic we need, however, to master not only one but all the elements, a fact that is absolutely correct from the magic standpoint. So much for this.*

Ray: Later when you have reached total mastership over the elements you will also be able to densify the energies to a material level for strong effects. For now and the next steps this degree is not necessary.
Absolutely necessary is to densify the elements down to the astral plane so that you can really feel them. Many students miss this point and do these exercises only on the mental plane and wonder about why they do not make real progress. So this is a must.

Bardon: *Let us now pass on to the exercises concerning the air element. What has been said about the fire element applies in the same way top the* *air element, but for the fact that a different imagination of the senses has to be considered. Take up the same comfortable position, close your eyes, and imagine yourself to be in the middle of a mass of air that is filling the whole universe. You must not perceive anything of your surroundings, and nothing should exist for you but the air- filled space embracing the whole universe. You are inhaling the air element into your empty vessel of the soul, and the material body thorough the whole-body breathing (with the lungs and pores). Every breath is filling the whole body to an increasing extent and with more air. You have got to hold fast the imagination of your body being filled with air by each breath in such a way that is resembles a balloon. Combine it at the same time with the imagination that your body is becoming lighter, as light as air itself. The sensation of lightness should be so intense that finally you do not feel your body at all. In the same way you did begin with the fire element, start now also with seven inhalations and exhalations. With this exercise done, you should again have the posi-tive feeling that not the smallest particle of the air element remains in your body, and consequently you should feel in the same normal condition as before. To avoid any counting, use the string of beads again. Increase the number of breaths (inspirations and expirations) from one exercise to the next, but do not exceed the number of forty. By constant practice of this experiment, adepts will succeed in producing phenomena of levitation such as walking on the surface of water, floating in the air, displacement of the body and many more, especially if one concentrates on one element only. But magician is not satisfied with one-sided phenomena, because this would not agree with his aims. He wants to penetrate far deeper into the cognition and the mastery, and achieve more. Now follow the description of the practice concerning the water element. Take up the position you are accustomed to by now, close your eyes, and forget all around you. Imagine the whole universe is an enormous ocean and you are in the centre of it. Your body becomes filled with this element with each whole-body breath. You should feel the cold of the water in your whole body. If you have filled up your body with this element in seven breaths, you should empty it with seven breaths. Not the smallest amount of water element should remain in you at the last exhalation. Here again the string of beads will be a great help to you. With each new exercise, take one more breath. The more often you practice this exercise, the more distinctly you will feel the cold proper-ties of the water element. You ought to feel, as it were, like a lump of ice. Each of the exercises should not exceed twenty minutes. As time goes by, you ought to be able to keep your body cold as ice even in the hottest* summer weather. Oriental adepts master this element in such a degree that they can perform the most astonishing phenomena straight away. For example, they produce rain during the hot or dry season, and stop it again at will. They can ban thunderstorms, calm down the roaring ocean, control all animals in the water, and so on. Such and similar phenomena are no miracles for a real magician who understands them perfectly. All that is left is the description of the last element, that of the earth. Take up your routine position as you did before. This time, imagine the whole universe being the earth with yourself sitting in the middle of it. But do not imagine the earth as a lump of clay, but being a dense earthy material. The specific property of this earthy material is density and gravity. Now you ought to fill your body with this heavy material. Begin again with seven breaths and increase one breath more with each new exercise. You must manage to concentrate so much of the earthy material into yourself that your body seems as heavy as a lump of lead and almost paralyzed by the weight. Breathing out happens in the same way as it did in the other exercises. At the end of this exercise you ought to feel as normal as before the beginning. The duration of this exercise also is limited to twenty minutes at the most. This exercise (sadhana) is practiced by a great deal of Tibetan lamas mostly in such a way that they begin meditating on a lump of clay, dissecting it and going on to meditate on it again. The genuine magician knows better how to approach this element in a much simpler way, and to master it without such a difficult meditation process. The color of the different elements may serve as a useful resort to imagination, as far as fire is red, the air is blue, water is greenish blue, and the earth yellow, gray or black. Color vision or sensation is quite individual, but not absolutely necessary. Anyone believing it to favor his work may make use of it in the beginning. What chiefly matters in our exercises is the sensory imagination. After a longer spell of exercises, everybody should be able, for example, to produce heat with the fire element in such a degree that it can be demonstrated with a thermometer as a fever heat. This preliminary exercise of element mastery needs to be given the utmost attention. The adept can produce manifold kinds of phenomena say by controlling the earth element, and it is left to everybody to meditate on this problem for himself. Mastery of the elements is the darkest chapter of magic about which very little has been said to date, because the greatest Arcanum is hidden in it. At the same time, however, it is the most important magical domain, and he who does not possess the elements will scarcely get on in magical science.

Ray: Please pay attention to your training room. When you do exercises with all kinds of energy it is not uncommon that you charge your room as a side effect. So from time to time or after each exercise you should let your room exhale all energies which are too much.

A room which is charged can influence you for example by making you nervous – too much tension for your nerves. Regard what Bardon says about being overcharged.

STEP III - MAGIC PHYSICAL TRAINING

1. RETAINING OF STEP I, WHICH HAS TO BECOME A HABIT

2. ACCUMULATION OF VITAL POWER

A. BY BREATHING THROUGH THE LUNGS & PORES IN THE WHOLE BODY

B. IN DIFFERENT PARTS OF THE BODY

3. IMPREGNATION OF SPACE FOR REASONS OF HEALTH, SUCCESS, ETC.

4. BIO-MAGNETISM

Bardon: The first step of this training course ought to have become second nature with you by now. Let us therefore go into greater detail here. The position of repose of the body is to be kept during half an hour.

Ray: Deep meditations respectively breathing exercises can take 30 – 45 – 60 minutes. So it makes certainly sense to be able to keep your physical body for at least half an hour in a calm and comfortable position to work without any disturbances on the higher planes. Half an hour is indeed a good time and in most cases enough. It certainly depends on the kind of meditation/ training you currently do.

Bardon: *The pore-breathing of the whole body now shall be limited to certain single organs. The beginner must be enabled to allow any part of his body to breathe at will through the pores. One begins with the feet and finishes with the head. The practice is as follows: Sit in your usual position and close your eyes. Transfer yourself with your consciousness into one of your legs.*

Ray: Something in general first: Although you might be able to perform an exercise, you shouldn´t go on directly. It is important that you practice an exercise over a certain period of time to attain the referring transforma-tion of your microcosm and with this a consolidation of your new ability. If you stop too early your exercises then your body can´t build a lasting good structure for this ability. This is comparable with all kinds of learning processes. It is never enough to be able to do something one time or two times. Repetition and training are necessary to set the ability for all times.
When Bardon speaks of transferring your consciousness then you might wonder what this means or how this works. Your consciousness, - mind is a principle of the Akasha which means that your mind is independent from time and space. A normal human is accustomed to being with his mind in the head region but indeed you can set your mind everywhere without limits. In these first exercises dealing with the transfer of your conscious-ness you can accomplish it by setting your sensation, your feeling into another region. For example you close your eyes and concentrate on the sensation of your right foot. With this you automatically set your mind into your right food (in parts) and you are able to sense what happens there. A bigger part of your mind keeps in the head and a smaller part is in your foot. The longer and the more intensive your concentration/meditation lasts the more consciousness is set into your foot. After a longer training of the transfer of consciousness you are able to set your mind completely in your foot and everywhere else. This will be the first good step for mental wandering.
At last, - a magician must be able to set his mind in all body regions and all organs to let them breathe, to work there. Certainly this is just a matter of training and time.
So just try! Doing an exercise instead of too much thinking about it is one major key to real success. Keep this in mind.

Bardon: *It will not matter whether you start with the right or left leg. Imagine your leg, like the lungs, inhaling and exhaling the vital force together with your pulmonary breath from the universe. Consequently the vital power is inhaled (sucked in) from the universe and exhaled (secreted) back into the universe. If you have succeeded in doing so, after seven breaths, turn to the other leg. Having been successful herein as well, start with your hands, taking one first, then the other hand in order to breathe, and later with both hands at the same time. If you have achieved the desired result, let us step up to the next organs. Such as the genitals, bowels, stomach, liver, lungs, heart, larynx and head.*

Ray: Regarding the organs it makes sense to look them up in a book or in the internet how they look like and where they can be found. In your exercise you can imagine the organ you want to work with without the rest of your body. Combine it with setting your consciousness, your sensation into the organ and then let it breath. Remember also that you operate on the astral plane where energy can access organs etc. easily (different to the physical plane). Bardon once said that it is all quite simple and he is certainly right with this statement. The whole magical training and philosophy is just a matter of changing your way to think and to understand creation.

Bardon: *The purpose of this exercise will be accomplished if you have got each organ of your body, even your smallest, to do the breathing. This exercise is all the more important as it gives us the opportunity of controlling each part of the body, charging it with vital power, healing and restoring it to life. If we have managed to all this on our own person, it is not difficult to act on other bodies by transference of consciousness, which fact consequently plays an important part in the magnetic power transference in the magic art of healing. Please pay the greatest attention to his exercise. Another exercise of magic body training is the accumulation of vital power. We have already learned how to inhale and exhale the vital power through whole body pore breathing. Now let us pass on to the accumulation of vital power. Its practice is as follows: Sit in your customary position and inhale the vital force out of the universe into your body, through the lungs and the pores of your whole body. This time, however, do not give back the vital power to the universe, but keep it in your body. When breathing out, do not think about anything at all, and breathe out the consumed air quite regularly and evenly. With each new breath you feel* *how you are inhaling more and more vital power, accumulating and storing it in your body. You need to feel the pressure of the vital force like compressed steam in yourself, and imagine the compressed vital power coming out of your body like heat waves from a radiator.*

Ray: Bardon´s comparison of accumulated energy with heat waves from a radiator doesn´t mean that vital energy is hot. It means that the compressed energy is radiating from your whole body. Indeed these are energetic rays vertically from the surface of your body. This is a natural phenomenon and serves as a protection to keep negative energies away from yourself. Therefore it is also called "health aura". So when you accumulate vital energy then you increase your natural radiation and with this your health aura and also your charisma and your ability to influence your surroundings and other people. Charisma means nothing else but radiation and a high energy level together with some special personal qualities.
It is truly a misunderstanding to think that vital energy is hot or golden like some people think. Vital energy is neutral as it contains the electric and the magnetic fluid. It appears in forms of very small spherules. The body uses this energy to create/ produce all kinds of special energies for the different functions within the human metabolism.
Never forget that all these energy exercises are independent form the physical world. So don´t try to breathe in with your physical body as this doesn´t work. It all takes place on the astral plane with different laws. Breathing of forms or organs is here no problem.

Bardon: *With every breath the forces of pressure and radiation increase, spreading out and strengthening by meters. After repeated exercises you must be able to emit your penetrating power even for miles. You must actually feel the pressure and penetration of your rays. Practice makes perfect! Begin by inhaling seven times and increasing by one inspiration each day. Each single exercise should be limited to twenty minutes at the most. These exercises have to be practiced mainly in such tasks and experiments as require a great and intense expenditure of vital force, say the treatment of sick people, telepathy, magnetizing of objects, and so on. If the vital power is no longer wanted in this accumulated form, the body must be brought back to its original tension, because it is not advisable to walk about in everyday life in an over dimensioned tension. It would overstrain the nerves and cause nervous irritation, exhaustion and other bad side effects. The experiment is broken off by giving the accumulated force* back to the universe through imagination while breathing out. By doing so you will inhale pure air only, and breathe out the tension of the vital force until attaining the sensation of equipoise. After a longer practice, the magician will succeed in rendering the vital force to the universe at once, as it were in an explosive manner similar to a bursting tire. This abrupt elimination should not be practiced before your body has got a certain resisting power. Having acquired a certain skill, you may go on to achieve the same experiment with the single parts of the body, slowly and step by step. Mainly specialize on your hands. Adepts do the same with their eyes, too; thus they can fascinate and get under the spell of their will not only one individual, but a great number of them, sometimes even crowds of people. A magician who can manage all this with his hands is then known for having blessing hands. The mystery of blessing or laying on of hands depends on this. The exercise of this stage will have answered its purpose if you have learned how to accumulate vital power not only in the whole body but in each single part of it, and to emit the rays of this accumulated force directly to the outside. When you master this exercise, the third stage of the magic physical training will be completed.

APPENDIX TO STEP III

Bardon: The scholar who has arrived at this point of his magic development will already observe a general transmutation of his individuality. His magic faculties will increase in all the spheres. As to the mental sphere, he will have attained a stronger willpower, greater resistance, a better memory, a keener observation, and a clear intellect. In the astral sphere, he will notice that he has become calmer and steadier and, according to his aptitudes, he will further develop the faculties still slumbering in him. In the material world, he will persuade himself that he feels healthier, fitter and sort of rejuvenated. His vital force will far surpass that of his fellow men and he will achieve a great deal in everyday life by means of his emissive power. For example, he will be able to free any room he is living in from unfavorable influences. He will be able to treat sick persons successfully, even at remote distances, because he can emit his rays for miles. Besides, his emissive force allows him to charge objects with his desire. The scholar then will find out for himself when and where he can best utilize his magical faculties. But he should never forget that magic powers can be used for *the good as well as for egoistic purposes. Remember the quotation: "Thou shall reap what thou hast sown". Always let your final goal be to do noble things and to make mankind better. The technique of magnetism presents all possible variations, of which we are going to show you some.*

Ray: At this stage you have already developed strong creative powers. They will help you to master your life and all other things with success. Your wishes will manifest easier and faster. So it is highly recommendable to be full aware of what you think and feel, of what you wish for as everything you think, feel and wish for has a strong tendency to realize itself. Now you bear a much higher responsibility for everything than normal people. To say it clearly: Only idiots hurt themselves with full awareness. So in fact you are not able any longer to behave in an evil without being punished quickly by the Lords of karma. To behave evil at this stage means to start digging your own grave. It means to reap bad fruits which you have to stomach. To make negative experiences in life is normal but here it has major consequences. In the worst case your spiritual support is withdrawn from you and Akasha itself leads you astray. This means for now the end of your development. Worst is when you are picked up from dark forces as you have to pay for all they do for you.

So in conclusion it makes much sense to be a genuine spiritual student who embodies the positive principle, the divine light to act lawful and in best way for God, mankind and creation. So use your creative powers to be a real blessing for everyone and a worthy agent of the eternal light.

As a real servant of God, mankind and creation you will receive much support from the spiritual realms to continue your development successfully to spiritual perfection. Selfish persons will never get the necessary support to master the spiritual path. A very big part of real progress depends on the love and grace of God and his agents. Like the Egyptians said, - your heart must be light like a feather to let you pass into heaven.

1. SPACE IMPREGNATION

Bardon: *Through pulmonary and pore breathing of your entire body, you inhale vital force, pressing it with all your imagination into your whole body so that it becomes as it were dynamically radiant. Your body is something like the radiant energy, an individual sun. With every inhalation you enforce the compressed vital power as well as the radiant energy, and fill* *the room you live in. With the aid of this radiant power, the room must be literally sunlit. With repeated and persistent exercise, it is even possible to illuminate the room in darkness or at night to such a degree that objects can be perceived not only by the experimenter by also by laymen, because it is possible in this way to materialize the light of the vital force in the form of real daylight, which properly speaking is a simple imagination exercise.*

Ray: Certainly it makes not much sense to focus now your training on manifesting daylight. We are not magicians on stage to show spectacular things for an astonished audience. Our aim should be to gain mastership and real transformation, - real development. Such special things like materializing daylight you can train if you have endless spare time or no better things to do. Indeed there are more important things to master and time is in general precious. Bardon spoke about this phenomenon just because it really exists. Later when you have reached a high degree of mastership with a high amount of repetitions in breathing and accumulating all kinds of energy then you do not need much additional training to do such special things. But at the moment it makes no sense.

Regarding the law of silence, one of the four pillars, you probably never will such phenomena to other people. In fact normal people see these things in a different way than spiritual students and masters. Magic and its application are not for curiosity but for serious intentions.

Bardon: *This phenomenon alone will not of course satisfy the magician, who knows that vital force has a universal character, being not only the carrier of his ideas, thoughts and desires, but also the realizer of his imagination, and that he can attain all things through this vital power. As for realization, it depends on the plastic imagination. If the experimenter has filled his work room with his radiant energy, he ought to imagine what he wishes to attain, e.g., that all astral or magic influences existent in the room shall disappear and dissolve, or the magician shall feel safe and sound in the room as well as all people coming in. Besides, the magician may impregnate his rooms with the desire of being benefited in all his works by inspiration, success, etc. Advanced magicians screen their rooms from unwelcome people by rendering them restless and uncomfortable as soon as they enter the room so that they leave, unwilling to remain in there. Such a room is loaded or impregnated with protective or alarming ideas. But it is possible to load any room in more subtle ways so that any-*

one who enters the room without permission will feel sort of paralyzed and repelled. You see, a magician is offered a lot of possibilities, and with the help of these instructions, you can find out other methods.

Ray: Certainly it makes sense to do experiments for all these purposes to gain own practical experiences. The technique of charging rooms with vital energy plus impregnating the energy with a certain program/purpose is very useful. You can give the rooms of your flat different tasks. For example one to restore your health and vitality, one to clear all negative influences of every person which comes in, one for perfect inspiration in everything you do, one for a deep relaxation, good dreams and a perfect sleep and so on. You can also charge your car for protection and a safe, happy driving. You can certainly also charge an imagined space in your garden for a good mood at a garden party or something like this. Health, stress release, good mood, inspiration, fortune, protection – all these things are very useful.

Bardon: *The magician can give back the accumulated vital virtue to the universe, when breathing out, leaving the radiant or illuminating force in the room only with the aid of his imagination. But through this same imagination he can also suggest the vital force from the universe directly to the room without accumulating it by his physical power, especially if he has got some practice in accumulating vital force. This way, he can impregnate a room even with his own desires. Imagination combined with willpower and faith and firm conviction knows no bounds.*

Ray: The last sentence is the major key for success in all operations.

Bardon: *These experiments of the magician do not depend on one definite room; he may impregnate two or more rooms at the same time, and load an entire house with his vital force and radiant energy, according to the aforesaid method. As imagination knows neither time nor space, he can do all this at the remotest distance. As time goes on and his technique improves, he will be able to load any room whatever and wherever. But with regard to his ethical development, he will never make the wrong use of his faculties, but do noble things only, and his power will be unlimited, for practice makes perfect.*

Ray: As an experiment, - if you have a special place where you like to go, maybe in nature or at the sea you can charge one of your rooms with the energetic atmosphere/quality of your beloved place. This can be quite amazing. Your room can provide for example the energetic quality of a forest, - fresh, healthy energy. It is also possible that you are able to smell and feel this energy. I recommend to make several experiments to grow in abilities and experiences.

1. BIOMAGNETISM

Bardon: Let us deal with another specific property of the vital energy that is of particular relevance for the magic work. As we have already seen, each object, each animal, each human being, each form of ideas can be charged with vital force and the corresponding desire of realization. The vital force, however, has the property of accepting any -- also strangers' -- ideas and feelings, influencing or combining them. The concentrated vital force would therefore soon mingle with other ideas, a fact that would reduce the effect of the impregnated idea or even scuttle it if the magician did not provoke a reinforced tension by frequent repetition, thus reviving the desire or the idea. Bu this often means loss of time and is not very favorable to the final success. The desired influence will persist only so far as the tension is effective in the desired direction. Then the vital fore will dissolve, mingle with other vibrations, and the effect fades away by and by. To prevent this, a magician ought to be well acquainted with the laws of biomagnetism.

Ray: As said before biomagnetism is just an old term for vital energy respectively the work of the electromagnetic fluid in a body. So the laws of biomagnetism are the laws of vital energy.

Bardon: The vital force accepts not only an idea, concept, thought or feeling, but also time- ideas. This law respecting this specific property of the vital virtue must be considered when working with it, or later on with the elements. Therefore, when impregnating desires with the aid of vital energy, remember time and space. In magic work you have to consider the following rules above all: Working in the Akasha principle is timeless and spaceless; in the mental sphere, you operate with time; in the astral sphere, you work with space (shape, color); in the material world, you work with time and space simultaneously. I am going to explain the functions of biomagnetism in the light of some examples. With the help of your vital force, charge a room with the desire that you feel well in it. Enthrall this force with the desire that, as long as you live in the room, the influence should persist, continue renewing, and keep doing so, even when you leave the room and are absent for some time.

Ray: Here he speaks about universal terms for the design of formulas: The energy/ influence should "persist, strengthen, renew... as long as....automatically... then it should dissolve itself in the universe...." So there are a few main components of formulas which are always the same for nearly all purposes. In his coming chapters he shows some more similar or completive components of formulas. It is recommendable to note them for your practical work. In general when you use a formula/ program for energy then answers yourself first the questions: Who, where, why, how, when, - also don´t forget to put conditions into the formulas. But also try to keep it as simple as possible.

Bardon: *Should anyone else enter your room ignoring that there is an accumulation of vital force, he will feel very uncomfortable in your dwelling. Now and again, you can reinforce the density and power of your radiant energy in your room by repeating the desire. If you live in a room influenced in such a favorable way, the stored vital force will always exert a good influence on your health, and consequently on your body. The vital force in this room has the desire vibration of the health. If, however, you intend to do occult exercises in this room which have nothing to do with health, following another thought vibration, you will not book the same good results as in an unloaded room or in a room that you have charged with a desire responsive to your idea. Therefore it is always advisable to load the room with the thought vibrations corresponding to your respective work and experiments.*

Ray: It is good to charge not all rooms respectively to keep your training room uncharged as you will do a lot of different exercises there. Maybe you choose an extra place only for meditations without any energy breathings. This place you can charge for divine inspiration and intuition, also for a clear understanding of all subjects you work on.

Bardon: *So for instance, you might charge a ring, a stone or any other object with the wish that the person wearing it should be favored by for-*

tune and success. Now there are two possibilities of fixing and timing. The first method consists in fixing the vital virtue on the stone or the metal with your imagination and your concentrated wish, timing it so that the force shall remain forever in it, drawing even further from the universe to bring fortune and success to the person concerned as soon as she will wear the object. You may, of course, load the object you choose for a short time only if you like, so that the influence is broken off as soon as the purpose aimed at is attained. The second possibility is called universal loading, which is operated in the same way, including, however, the concentrated wish that as long a time as the object (ring, stone, jewelry) exists, the bearer of it should be benefited by fortune, success, etc. Such universal loadings performed by an adept will keep their virtues and their effects for centuries. As we have learned from the history of the Egyptian mummies, such fixed forces continue acting for thousands of years. If a talisman or an object destined and individually loaded for a definite person falls into the hands of someone else, he will not experience the least influence. But if this object returns to the true owner, this influence will go on acting. Now let me describe another field where vital force is active, namely that of healing magnetism. If a magician treats a sick person, no matter whether personally by magnetic strokes or by putting on hands, or at a distance, i.e., by imagination and willpower, he must the law of time exactly if he wants to be successful.

Ray: Here are some more components and conditions for the design of formulas. It is good to meditate about the differences and the possibilities of using these components and formulas.
"Magnetic strokes" is also a term of former times. It means that you emit vital energy from your hands by stroking over the body of the patient. So indeed you charge the patient through your hands. This should be done only with charged hands otherwise you lose your own energy which is not preferable.

Bardon: *The routine manner of magnetizing is as follows: The magnetizer, with the aid of imagination, makes his vital force flow out of his body, mostly from his hands, into the sick person. This method supposes the magnetizer to be positively sound and to have a surplus of vital force, or else he will bring danger into his own health. I am sorry to say that I have seen bad cases where the magnetizer, by excessive transfers of his own vital force, suffered such heavy damage to his health that he faced a com-*

plete nervous breakdown, apart from other side effects such as diseases of the heart, and so on. Such consequences are unavoidable if the magnetizer spends more force than he is able to restore, especially if he is treating several patients at once. This method presents another disadvantage, namely that the magnetizer uses his own force to transfer his own psychic vibrations and character traits onto the patient, influencing him indirectly in a psychic way too. Therefore, every magnetizer is supposed and required to be of a noble character. Yet if a magnetizer has a patient whose character properties are worse than his own, he will indirectly draw the evil influences of the patient on himself, which is disadvantageous for the magnetizer in any event. The magnetizer who, however, has been trained in occultism does not give the patient all of the vital force of his own body, but draws it from the universe and makes it stream into the patient's body directly through his hands, together with the concentrated desire of health. With both methods, magnetizing has to be repeated often if one wants a quicker success, for disharmony or diseases suck in and consume the transferred force very rapidly and are greedy for a further supply of force, so that the treatment has to be repeated soon to prevent the state from getting worse.

Ray: Healing treatments are an interesting subject. If you work in this direction, maybe also for yourself, then I recommend to charge the room or the whole flat of the ill person with a good amount of vital energy and to tell the energy to stabilize, to renew and to strengthen automatically from the universe until the person is completely healed. Tell it to dissolve all negative energies and to support all healing processes of the person. The person is supposed to feel better day by day. After the successful healing the energy is supposed to dissolve into the universe automatically. Certainly you should recharge the rooms additionally by yourself all three days. This is for better results.

Another or an additional treatment is to charge water for drinking. Water is really good to use for such purposes. I wouldn't charge meals in this case as it can be too much for digesting.

It is recommendable to make your own experiments in all aspects. You must be able to know how things work and how it feels for example to eat charged food. You should experience also the differences in the amount of charging. The higher something is charged the stronger are the results, sometimes things can be charged too strong to eat/drink without unwished side effects. It is also possible that an ill person receives your vital energy and then aches or other symptoms increase suddenly. Normally this is only for a short time but sometimes it can last longer and might be dangerous (heavy symptoms). This is the case at heavy diseases and very weak patients. In general a short increase of symptoms is a clear and positive sign that you have pushed the self-healing processes in the body. It is possible that you have to give another charge directly to support the healing process continuously.

In conclusion these healing treatments should be done with full awareness and responsibility. A spiritual student should make good experiences here as it is an important part of the magical education. We should be able to heal ourselves, our beloved ones, people in need, also animals and plants in need. The divine love is all-embracing.

Don't forget to ask your spiritual guide for assistance and inspiration before you do such operations. This makes the whole work safer. Also don't forget that daring is one of the four pillars. You will experience that there are many things you have to dare on the path. Without courage you can't accomplish your spiritual adventure.

By the way I have survived everything so far although I had to think twice often. Dangers and risks are a quality of life. With the right spiritual attitude you master all challenges, equal how they look like. Just be tough like a Samurai. This helps. ;-)

Bardon: *It is otherwise with the magician. The patient feels relieved only when the magician has been psychically opened, i.e., if he has accomplished a dynamic accumulation of vital force in his own body and emits light rays of vital force. The magician can employ many methods successfully, but he must always maintain the imagination combined with the desire concentration, wishing that the patient gets better and better, hour by hour, from day to day. Some methods will follow, the use of which will help a magician in the treatment of diseases. Above all, he must be well versed in the diagnosis of diseases and their symptoms. He will gain this knowledge through a careful study of the respective literature. Anatomical knowledge is absolutely indispensable. He will not be so careless as to treat diseases necessitating a rapid chirurgical intervention, or infectious diseases. But in such cases he will be able to accelerate the healing process and contribute to soothing the pains, besides the medical treatment. He can manage doing so even at a distance.*

Ray: Healing on distance is the same but completely depending on your imagination. Here you use the Akasha principle which means that you switch off time and space and work as the patient is directly in front of you. Indeed the whole magical work is a matter of imagination. You do not depend on space and time. There are neither unbridgeable distances nor obstacles.

Bardon: *It would be very serviceable if physicians specialized in this field and, besides the allopathic art, learned to employ the magic practice. Therefore the magician should only treat such sick persons as are recommended for this kind of treatment directly by a physician, or work together with a physician to avoid being regarded as a quack or a charlatan. He should follow his calling from pure love of his neighbors and not for the purpose of earning money or as a means of enriching himself. Do not climb upwards on the credulities of mankind. Hold on to the ideal of goodness, and blessing will not fail. Ideally colored magicians will help sick persons without them knowing anything. This kind of help is the most blissful.*

Ray: According to the law of silence it can be quite dangerous and aggravating to proclaim that you are a magician and that you can heal people. So all kinds of treatments with vital energy etc. should be done very considerately and carefully. Remember the burning of witches in former days. This exists still today but in a different form. If you don't want to be marked as a candidate for a madhouse with all negative consequences then keep the law of silence. Treat people only directly when you know them and they accept you as a spiritual person. Maybe you can also cover your treatment under a different accepted name. Hurting laws like the law of silence can result in a painful punishment. But after such an experience you have learned your lesson.
Helping/treating people without their knowledge is indeed very blissful. It is a part of Karma Yoga which helps you to make good progress in your development and also to dissolve your own bad karma.

Bardon: *Let me add some of the most conventional methods a magician can make use of without endangering his health and nervous system. Before approaching a sick person's bed, do at least seven breaths through the lungs and pores; accumulate an enormous amount of vital force, drawing it from the universe into your body, and let this vital force shine like brightest light of the sun. By repeated inhaling of the vital force, try to produce a* *radiant energy of at least ten yards around your body, which corresponds to a vital force of ten normal persons. You ought to feel as if your accumulated vital force were lighting up like a sun. If you approach a patient with such a radiance, he will instantly feel a relief, a sensation of ease, and if not afflicted by too painful an illness, he will feel an immediate alleviation. You transfer the accumulated radiant energy quite individually to the patient and it is up to you to act as you like. A skilled magician needs no magic strokes nor laying on of hands, all that being only auxiliary manipulations, supports for the utterance of his will. He may keep his eyes open or closed during this operation. If he wants, he may look straight at the patient, but he need not do it directly. Here it is exclusively the imagination that is working. But during the whole act of power transference, the magician may also sit with the patient without contacting him personally. Imagine that the radiant energy surrounding you will stream forth into the patient's body and be pressed into it, penetrating and illuminating all the pores of the sick person. Let your will power order the compressed radiant energy to bring about the recovery of the patient. All the time you have to be absolutely convinced that the patient is feeling better from one hour to the next, that he does look better every day, and you must also order the radiant energy not to escape from the body before the patient has fully recovered. Loading the body of a patient quantitatively with the radiant energy which in a sound person means a range of one yard, you will be able to bring about recovery in a surprisingly short time in proportion to the kind of illness. Repeat the loading after a while; reinforce the tension of the concentrated radiant energy, and you will be very surprised indeed at noticing the wonderful success you have accomplished. First of all, the radiant energy cannot escape because you fixed it, ordering of to renew itself constantly. Secondly, you fixed the time so that the body should feel better from hour to hour, from day to day, and thirdly, you have proportioned the power to the space corresponding to the circumference of the body. At his point, it should be recommended to fix the power of radiation at about one yard outside the body, which is equal to the radiation of a normal human being. With this method you have now fulfilled the main condition of the material law of time and space.*

Ray: Here Bardon describes again main aspects of formulas and general techniques concerning the work with energy.

The use of light is a very powerful healing technique. The body can use light directly without having to transform it (like it has to with vital energy). So light can bring direct relief when the patient has aches and it is recommendable when the patient is very weak. Certainly you can use light in general for healing. These things are up to you.

Bardon: *While using this method, the magician will notice that his radiant energy which he transferred to the patient does not diminish, but keeps on lighting up in the same intensive manner as before. This is to impute to the fact that the vital power accumulated in the body renews itself automatically, similar to communicating pipes, instantly replacing the radiated power. Therefore it is obvious that a magician is able to treat hundreds of patients without ruining his mental strength or his nerves. A different method has to be used if the magician is pressing the vital power directly into the patient's body or into the sick part of the body, only by way of the pores together with the imagination of renewing itself constantly from the universe, till the moment of complete recovery is reached. Here the imagined desire of complete recovery is limited to tie and space as well. But this method is only practiced with patients whose nervous system is not yet wholly exhausted, and can consequently bear a certain pressure of the accumulated vital power. With a well-trained magician, of course, the accumulated vital power is, as it were, materialized already, meaning that it is condensed material power that can be compared to electricity. This method, in comparison with the others, is the most popular because it is very simple and exceedingly effective. A very peculiar method is to let the patient inhale one's own radiant power emanation with the help of the imagination. Presuming the patient to be able to concentrate, he can do so himself; otherwise, the magician has to perform the imagination instead of the patient. In practice the occurrence is as follows: Your radiant energy is emitting up to a range of 10 yards. As you are near the patient, he is actually swimming in the light of your radiation, which has been impregnated with the desire of recovery. The patient on whom this power has been concentrated will be firmly convinced that he is inhaling your radiant energy with every breath, and will get well. He must imagine intensely that he will go on feeling better and better, even when the magician will no longer be near him. Presuming the patient to be unable to concentrate or, in the case of sick children, you imagine yourself that with every inhalation the patient accepts your own radiation of vital power, conveys it to the blood, and will bring about a complete recovery. Here also you will have to concentrate on the wish that the force inhaled by the patient should keep on working positively in him. This has been an example of vital force transfe-*

rence from the magician's to another's body by breathing. We can rely on the word of the Bible, when our Lord Jesus Christ was touched by a sick woman in the hope of recovery. Our Lord felt the diminution of his vital power and he remarked to his disciples, "I have been touched!"

Ray: The experience Jesus made can everyone repeat or experience by himself. When a well trained student of magic is touched by a person with a low level of vital energy, the energy of the student transfers automatically to increase the level of the weak person. You can really feel how your own energy level is decreasing suddenly. The other person feels certainly immediately much better. Such a transfer of energy can be examined in many different cases, for example between man and woman or old people and young ones, etc.

In your own practice you will experience that the simple techniques are the preferred ones. Maybe you have witnessed "healers" or "masters" who made a great fuss with strange rituals and chanting or whatever. A real master does not need a great fuss or complicated rituals for successful treatments and magical operations. A big show is not necessary, also not really helpful. Certainly there exist many possibilities to treat people like Bardon describes. It is also recommendable to try all techniques of Bardon to increase your abilities and your understanding of the matter. Practical experiences are most important.

Bardon: *Working with vital power and magnetism, one has to consider time and space. With a view to this fact, I have quoted several examples concerning the treatment of diseases, and I could still mention quite a number of methods for treating sick people from the magnetic standpoint. For example, the magician is able to take up a connection with the mind of a sleeping patient and to realize various methods of treatment in the patient's body. Apart from treating the sick with vital power, he can also cure them magically with the help of the elements, magnetism, and electricity. The detailed description of all the methods and possibilities of treatments would certainly fill a very voluminous book. In this work I am only going to point out single procedures of treatment with regard to time and space, that is magnetism.*

Ray: Magnetism means biomagnetism here – certainly. Another different or better term for biomagnetism is the tetrapolar magnet respectively the function/work of it. Details you can derive from his descriptions of the four elements and from your own experiences with the elements.

Bardon: *High adepts and saints who have trained their imagination to such perfection that all their imageries are realized immediately in all planes do not need methods any more. Such people have only to express any kind of desire and it will be realized at the very same moment.*

Ray: It sounds quite boring to do not need any methods. ;-)

Back to seriousness. High adepts are comparable to superior power stations while normal people are like small batteries. So it is no wonder that they provide such enormous powers to realize their wishes directly. One aspect of this is also their divine authority in creation which supports all their actions.

I stop here with my commentaries as this should be enough to help you mastering the entry of Bardon´s universal training. I hope my comments were useful to increase your understanding of the matter and to prevent you from eventual misunderstandings or traps.

WHAT BARDON DIDN´T SAY

Bardon has orientated his teachings and descriptions on the first Tarot Card. So he unveiled certainly everything what could be unveiled concerning this first side of the book of wisdom. But as you have probably noticed by reading his book the topics could easily fill at least a dozen big books. Unfortunately we have to master the path without them.

Bardon also focused only on the absolutely indispensable techniques and teachings. So many helpful explanations and descriptions are missing. The consequence is that students have to study a lot of additional books to get a better impression of what he is talking about. To get the right stuff for deeper studies divine guidance is absolutely necessary as the high quality teachings are very rare and a lot of misleading books are on the market.

Bardon described all points of the science and art of magic. But magic is just one side of a greater whole. So the main and most important thing Bardon didn´t speak about is mysticism, the other, completive side of magic. Mysticism gives magic quality, intention, beauty, etc. Mysticism describes the path of transformation from a normal human being to a temple of God, to a divine expression, to a real son/daughter of God, a real brother/sister of the eternal light, indeed to a cosmic being. Mysticism starts with the deep spiritual desire to grow, to find God, to unite with God in love, to serve God and creation, to do the right things, to follows the divine laws. Magic is the instrument to accomplish the mystical union in all aspects, in absolute perfection. Without the magical development we are neither able to experience God completely nor to express him in perfection. So indeed mysticism in its right understanding is absolutely necessary to master the path. Bardon presumes that the reader, student is already a mystic, at least so far that he has a strong spiritual desire. So indeed the mystical attitude, - the right spiritual attitude is absolutely necessary for real progress on the magical path. Magic and mysticism are the two sides of the one path to spiritual perfection. Unfortunately there are many readers who are just looking for gaining magical powers. This can´t work. By the way the highest and greatest form of mystical training is presented by Bardon in his third book about Quabbalah. Blessed is the one who is allowed to accomplish this training.

In general Bardon "loves" to give very small hints about major topics. Sometimes his hints are mentioned only once in one single sentence or in a subordinate clause. In this way he hinted at mysticism and also on the topics like health and activating the chakras.

He said that it is a basic requirement to be in total health to master the path. I can only emphasize this. All kinds of imbalances on mental, astral (soul) and physical plane are obstacles which make it difficult to proceed. So indeed it is necessary to balance you as far as possible to start and to make good progress. I recommend to consult healers when you have health problems before you really start the practice, especially with energetic breathing techniques, to balance you. Balance is one high aim on the path. Clear and heal yourself before and everything will be easier. In cases where it is quite difficult to heal yourself you can certainly do the training anyway but you need much more time and will power to make progress. In fact when you practice the exercises successfully you will experience that they have a clearing, healing and balancing effect on you. You will benefit from all exercises in all aspects of your personality and in your life. In fact no one and nothing is able to stop a genuine spiritual seeker.

About the chakras he says that they are psychic centers and that one can activate them with reference to Gregorius and his book about activating the chakras. This is not really much. Chakras are in fact the main and easiest key to access the spiritual realms, to start the spiritual development. Imagine that the whole universe with all spheres, qualities and powers is represented by maybe ten main chakras. So you are able to access the cosmos by using your chakras as they potentially provide all cosmic energies, powers, qualities and abilities. Regarding this fact all spiritual traditions have been working with them to initiate the transformation of their aspirants. The so called Kundalini Yoga was a part of the spiritual training in old Egypt. Now it is only known from India. Kundalini Yoga has the aim to activate all chakras with the serpent power sleeping in the root chakra.

It is the female creative power, the Shakti or Kundalini Shakti which rises from the bottom of the spine up to the crown chakra to unite with her lover Shiva. This can be seen on the first Tarot Card. Today Kundalini Yoga is a matter of getting the right initiation. Most of the Yogis of today have a only a very low level of initiation so there is not much progress to expect. As a magician and initiate in Pranic healing by Choa Kok Sui you can optimize the Kundalini Yoga training in best way. In my books I present useful techniques for the awakening of the chakras for a diversity of purposes. The direct work on awakening the Shakti in the root chakra should be done very carefully as negative side effects can occur. So when you want to do such things inform yourself well or do the safer training which I present. There the Shakti will be awakened indirectly. The Shakti is certainly nothing else than the power of imagination which Bardon intends to cultivate. So you see that all pretended different spiritual traditions are all based one eternal understanding of the human evolution. The eternal clothes itself in the different times, religions and cultural contexts but it remains the eternal truth.

The book of Gregorius is not recommendable for practice as it is not refined in its instructions. Gregorius himself and many other so called magicians are not recommendable to study as they worked in a way which is hair-raising. Most of them are ensnared in a mixture of egoism, illusions, dangerous, evil experiments, control and manipulation of others, etc. There is really better stuff for studies.

EPILOGUE

The magical art and with this the mystical transformation has to be experienced practically. Intellectual studies do not provide any transformation or progress or magical abilities. So the key is that you have to do it. Most people have dreams which they think about but never realize. So as simple as true stop dreaming and start your practice! This is the key for changes!

Franz Bardon, the great initiate, showed with his three main books the path to perfection, the path of the human evolution with all mile stones. Meanwhile all spiritual traditions have unveiled their inner teachings to support the progress of mankind. So in fact all doors are open for the genuine spiritual seekers to fulfill his desires, to reach his holy aims.

As Bardon says: "The disciple has to make the first part of the way and God meets him halfway."

Be blessed, my fellow on the path!

In love, light and service,

Ray del Sole

CONTACT:

Dear Reader,

if you like to contact me, please regard the following:

I can only provide answers for genuine spiritual seekers on the path – not for curiosity. Before you ask me try first to answer your question by own research as many questions of beginners and advanced students are already answered in my books and in the recommended spiritual literature.

Please respect that

- I have not much time for answering questions. I am very busy.
- I do not provide any magical help in any case. There are others who provide direct support.
- everyone has to go through the spiritual training by himself as training means a deep transformation of your personality, - there is simply no alternative. Discipline in training will let you reach all aims. Practice makes perfect!
- I am not interested in joining any kinds of circles, secret societies, brotherhoods etc.
- I am a genuine servant of the eternal light and only responsible to God, not to any kind of limited religion or human interests.

If you are interested in taking part in altruistic projects led by me in the future then you can mail me your name and email address and I will inform you when my projects start.

Further books of me are published on http://stores.lulu.com/raydelsole

Please mail to: raydelsole@yahoo.de

Thank you for your understanding.

In love, light and service,

Ray del Sole

About the author:

I am an architect with special skills in management, eco-biology and eco-nomics. I have visited many foreign countries so that I got to know the beautiful diversity of cultures and people. I am a cosmopolitan and I feel at home especially in the south and the east of the world. I feel the old bonds of former incarnations to other countries, forms of old love and apprecia-tion.

When I was a little child I have dedicated myself to the aim of understand-ing the world completely, how everything works. Today I would say – to understand God, man and creation, to gain real wisdom. So I started very early to study books about sciences, mysteries, religions, cultures, ancient history and spiritual teachings. Around the age of eighteen I began with the spiritual training system of Bardon. Indeed I chose this life to make as much spiritual progress as possible. And with this I will continue until I leave the material plane. For the future I have some spiritual, altruistic projects in mind. Let´s see what the coming years will bring.

Yours, Ray

27869878R00046

Made in the USA
Lexington, KY
26 November 2013